BA - 47

© 2014

P.S. WINN

Other titles by P.S. Winn

Foretold
Voices
Obligations
Tunnels
Capernicious
Stretched Stories

Available on Amazon books
http://www.amazon.com/author/pswinn

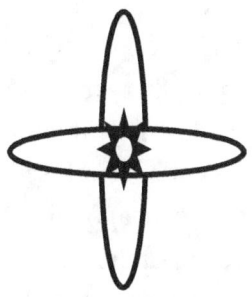

BA-47

Chapter 1

As the door flew open the feeling of déjà vu that came with the moment was overwhelming. It was so strong that Jack Carlton thought he would drown as the dark memory of that other time drug him into its deep depths. The last time this same thing had happened flew through his confused mind.
That had been three years ago, but still the similarities were remarkable.
That day a man had also stood in the bars' doorway. Today the morning sun on this almost summer day cast a glow that surrounded the man like an aura. A few specks of dust sparkled as they floated down in the air. Jack frowned as the man closed the door and stepped in to his bar.
The last time this had happened the man at the door had been Ed Sorenson. He was the owner of the local grocery store, if you could even call it that.
It was more of a mini market that the people of the subdivision loved for its convenience. Although they were only five or six miles from town, no one wanted to drive that far for just a forgotten jug of milk.

The man today was not Ed, but Jack still knew in his heart this man would utter those same words Ed had three years ago. Jack braced himself and waited.

Instead of saying "Rusty needs you, something is wrong." The words this man spoke hit Jack just as hard. "There's been an accident at the plant, Doctor Hardell sent me."

Jack just stared a moment as he let the words set in. Not Rusty then, of course not, his wife had passed away three years ago. But it was what happened on that day that had brought on this whole déjà vu thing that Jack had first met Bryan Hardell...

Jack had been alone at the bar and was standing behind the horseshoe shaped bar and wiping it down with a rag when the door flew open and his whole life changed. After Ed Sorenson had said something was wrong with Rusty, Jack had thrown down the bar rag and run out of the bar. He hadn't bothered waiting for Ed. Jack ran past the hardware store that stood next to the bar and straight to the grocery store where Rusty worked part time. The two had bought the bar from Rusty's Uncle for a song when he retired. They were just beginning to make ends meet, so Rusty had been working a few hours a week at the grocery store for extra spending money.

When Jack entered he saw Rusty sitting on a chair with her head down. Ann Sorenson hovered over her with a look of worry on her face. She looked up when Jack came in. "Jack, am I glad to see you. I don't know what happened, Rusty just let out a scream and grabbed her stomach. One look at her and I moved her to this chair, I thought she was going to pass out. Once she sat down she was a little better though."

Jack just nodded and went over to kneel in front of Rusty. He pushed her long red hair away from her face with a trembling hand. Jack put a hand under her chin and lifted her head so he could look into the brown eyes that he knew so well. He could see the pain in them and his heart ached. "What happened Rusty, what's wrong?"

Rusty gave Jack a weak smile. "The pain, oh God it hurts." Rusty winced as she tried to shift in her seat.

Jack put a hand on his wife's shoulder. "You just sit here, I'm calling an ambulance."

From there everything was a blur in Jack's mind. Following the ambulance carrying his wife to Bremerton where the hospital was. After that the hospital and the hours of testing, followed by days waiting for the results. Then came the two words spoken by the doctor that changed everything. "Pancreatic cancer."

Three months later Jack Carlton buried the love of his life. His best friend, his business partner, his whole life for the last ten years was gone at the young age of 36. Strangely enough it was the doctor who had given him the bad news to begin with who now became Jack's shoulder to lean on. They had become friends because of the awful tragedy.

At the time Bryan had lived in Bremerton, but when Bio Fuel Technologies opened their plant in the Garden Vista subdivision they had also built a small clinic. Dr. Hardell had applied for and gotten the job of running the clinic. Now he lived a block from the clinic and kitty corner from Jack's bar with the apartment in the back. That's why when the young man that had stormed into the bar this morning had said Dr. Hardell needed him, Jack didn't hesitate. Jack frowned at the young man now as he gripped the side of the bar. He felt like a kid that had just stepped off of a merry-go-round. The feel of the hard wood beneath his hand helped to steady Jack's nerves and slow his whirling thoughts.

Nodding, Jack stepped over to the kid. "Are you Bob Grady's boy?"

The young man nodded. "I'm Phillip and yeah, Bob's my dad. We own the hardware store next door."

Jack shook his head. "Sorry Phillip, I was just a little confused for a moment there. Now, what's wrong at the plant?"

Phillip shrugged. "I think you better talk to Dr. Hardell about that. He just said to come and get you and ask if you would bring your truck."

Nodding Jack started to step toward the front door patting his pocket to make sure his keys were there. "Okay Phillip, I'll follow you."

The two stepped out into the sunshine. Jack saw a small Chevy parked in front of the bar. He pointed at it. "This your car Phillip?"

The young man nodded. "Yeah, I just got it and by the way, you can call me Phil."

Smiling, jack nodded. "Okay Phil, my truck is around back, just give me a minute."

Jack walked around to the back of the bar and got in his half-ton black Dodge pick-up. He rolled down the windows surprised at how warm the cab already was. He looked at his watch, ten A.M. It was going to be another hot day and still two weeks until summer officially arrived.

Jack drove around to the front of the bar and then followed Phil the half-mile out to Bio Fuel Technologies or BFT as everyone called the plant.

As they pulled up to the front of the building Jack could see about a dozen people on the cement steps. Half were sitting and half were standing, but all had that gazed over look in their eyes of someone in shock. Jack was shaking his head as he got out of the truck. What the hell was going on?
Phil stepped up next to him. The young man was a good four inches taller than Jack's 5'10", and probably at least ten pounds lighter. If the boy filled out like his old man he'd make a good football player. Right now Phil was pretty thin and also looking pretty nervous.

"Dr. Hardell is inside."

Jack followed Phil up the six cement steps at the front of the building past the people gathered there. Jack was surprised that none of them seem to even notice him and Phil as they walked by. He was even more surprised when they stepped through the double glass doors into the empty lobby. Jack had expected the inside of the plant to be cooler than it was outside. If anything it was a degree or two warmer inside than out.

Phil pointed at a hallway just ahead of them. "The doctor is down there."

The two walked down the hall to the first room with an open door. Stepping in Jack figured the room must be some kind of break room for the plant's workers. Two women sat at a round table, one with her foot up on a chair. Her shoe was off and her foot had been wrapped in what looked like an ace bandage. Jack recognized the young woman as a bar customer. The other woman at the table was one of Bryan's nurses. Jack thought her name was Crystal. He looked across the room where he saw Bryan's other nurse. She was sitting next to a couch where an older gentleman was lying. His eyes were closed and he looked deathly white. Jack didn't think the nurse looked too much better. The man standing next to them turned when Jack and Phil entered the room.

"Jack, glad you're here." Bryan looked at Phil. "Thanks for bringing him back so quick."

Phil smiled and nodded as Jack stepped over to Bryan. "What the hell's going on here Bryan? What's going on with those people out front?"

Bryan pointed over to the corner of the room where a man Jack hadn't noticed before was standing up and sliding back the chair he had been sitting on. The man was about the same height as Jack, but about twenty pounds heavier and maybe ten years older than Jack's 42.

The dark haired man adjusted his glasses nervously and then stepped forward. "I don't know if I can tell you too much either. I was actually outside when it happened. I had just gone out to get some papers from my car."

Jack frowned. "Hold up a second, when what happened? Do you guys want to give me a clue as to what is going on here?" Jack looked at the professor and then back at Bryan.

The professor cleared his throat. "It was an accident in the lab. A chemical explosion, somehow...someone..."

The man took off his glasses and wiped his eyes before putting his glasses back on. "Dead, they're all dead."

Jack stepped another step closer to the professor. "Who's dead, make some sense."

The professor let out a deep sigh. "Twenty three of my co-workers are dead. Something happened, like I said I was outside. I had to get those files from my trunk. That's when I heard the siren and then heard this clanking noise as the fail safe shut down started."

Shaking his head Jack stepped closer, he and the professor were almost face to face now. "What is the fail safe shutdown?"

The professor looked at Jack, his green eyes huge behind his thick glasses. "It's a precaution that was built in at the plant. In the event of an accident the computer sensors would pick up any biohazard in the air and shut down the lab side of the plant. They are highly sensitive of course. When the sensors pick something up they are programmed to shut everything down to prevent exposure."

The professor shook his head again. "Dead, all dead."

Jack turned to Bryan. "What happened here Bryan? This guy isn't making any sense."

Bryan looked at the woman who was seated next to the older man on the couch. "Nancy, can you keep an eye on Mr. Everett for a minute?"

Nancy nodded and patted the man's shoulder. "Don't worry, I'll watch him."

Bryan nodded, turning to Jack. "I think it would be easier to show you than to explain."

Jack followed Bryan out of the room. The professor and Phil also followed Bryan and Jack up the hall and across to a small room.

They stepped inside to what looked like a computer room. The first thing that Jack noticed was a dark colored window about two feet square.

Bryan pointed at the square. "That looks out in to the lab. Go ahead and take a look, but be ready for a shock."

Jack stepped up to the window. As his eyes adjusted to the darker interior of the room they also widened in surprise. People, most in white lab coats seemed to be sprawled everywhere. Some had fallen to the floor while others had collapsed onto tables and over chairs. At first look they appeared to only be sleeping, but as Jack studied the room it became apparent these people were not just asleep. Jack could see spots of blood everywhere; it trickled from open mouths, noses and even from the ears of these poor people. No one in the closed lab was moving. Jack turned to the others. "Are you sure they are all dead? What if someone in there is somehow alive?"

Bryan shook his head. "I don't think so Jack. I've been checking about every fifteen minutes since I got here, no one in there has moved."

The professor cleared his throat. "You can't get in there anyway. The lab is now on lockdown. No one can go in." The professor turned with those words and walked out of the room.

Jack took a deep breath and looked at Bryan. "What about that old guy and that woman who had her foot up? What happened to them?"

Bryan pointed to the one empty chair in the room. "That was Mr. Everett's chair. His job was to monitor the lab. I think when this shut down happened and he saw what was really going on in there, he had a heart attack. The woman, Julie Warren, got pushed around when people panicked and started evacuating. Luckily all she got was a broken ankle. They really didn't even need to leave this side of the building. Once that computer shut down the lab, nothing could get out of there. Even the air conditioning and other vents have shut down."

Jack nodded, that's why it felt warm in here. Jack looked at Bryan shaking his head. "Why haven't I heard any sirens? Didn't you call an ambulance from Bremerton?"

Frowning, Bryan shook his head. "I tried, but I can't. It seems the landline phones are down and no one has been able to get a signal on their cell phones either."

Now Jack was frowning. "That's weird, what would cause that?"

Bryan shrugged. "I don't know maybe a problem with a cell tower somewhere. Right now all I want to worry about is moving Julie and Mr. Everett to the clinic. That's why I wanted you to bring your truck. I thought we could use it to move Mr. Everett."

Jack was still trying to get the morning's events to register and make some kind of sense in his head. He supposed that too could wait. Bryan was right they needed to take care of the two people that were in the other room first. "Okay Bryan, let's go do this."

Chapter 2

An hour later Julie Warren with her ankle in a cast was driven home by Phil. Jack and Bryan stood in front of the Bryan's clinic. They had told all the workers to leave the plant and just head home and they'd be in contact as soon as they could. Jack pulled a wrinkled pack of cigarettes from his shirt pocket. Bryan shook his head of dark hair. "I thought you quit?"

As he lit his smoke, Jack nodded. "I did quit. It just seems no matter how many times I quit the number of times I start up again is always one more."

Bryan laughed. "Guess I can't blame you after a morning like today. I just can't believe this, twenty three people, dead, just like that."
Bryan snapped his fingers and looked at Jack. "Mr. Everett isn't too far behind them either. He should be in a hospital. We got him to the clinic, but it just isn't set up for something major like that."
Bryan put a hand on Jack's shoulder. "I wonder if you will do something for me, you and Phil when he gets back."

Jack nodded. "What are you thinking Bryan?"

Letting out a breath, Bryan sighed. "I'd like the two of you to head over to Bremerton and get an ambulance out here. I'd go, but I need to watch my patient."

Jack nodded. "I'd be glad to do it. I need to try and find someone to report this accident or whatever the hell it was to. I can't believe someone hasn't shown up here already. I mean all that fancy, high tech equipment up to that plant. I'm sure somewhere there must be some red flags going off. Someone must know about this."

Bryan looked curiously at Jack. "That is strange isn't it? Maybe Evan would know something about that."

Jack frowned. "Who the hell is Evan?"

Bryan laughed. "He's the professor sitting back in my waiting room."

Taking a drag from his smoke Jack shrugged. "I think I like calling him professor better than Evan. I don't really trust him or anyone else involved with BFT. Not after this morning."

Both men looked up as Phil pulled in and stepped out of his car. Jack smiled. "Hey Phil, how'd you like to take a ride?"

Phil smiled. "Sure, can I drive?"

Laughing, Jack nodded, and then he bent down and put out his cigarette. He stood up holding the cigarette butt in his fingers, looking for a place to get rid of it. Bryan held out his hand. "Here, I'll throw it away for you."

Jack handed the butt to Bryan. "You should really have some kind of ashtray out here."

Bryan shook his head. "I don't encourage my patients to smoke."

Jack laughed. "Good thing I'm not your patient then." Jack turned to Phil. "You ready for that ride?"

Phil nodded. "Where we goin'?"

Jack walked over and opened the car door. "We're going to Bremerton to get an ambulance and then maybe some answers."

Jack and Phil left in the young man's car and Bryan went back into the clinic to check on his patient.

With Phil driving, he and Jack headed east out of the subdivision toward the town of Bremerton. Jack looked over at Phil. "I'm sorry I didn't recognize you earlier in the bar. I was confused for a minute there." Jack didn't have any explanation for that confusion so he didn't elaborate.

Phil was laughing. "Hey, don't worry; this whole day has been confusing for me. Besides I have been away to college. I just graduated."

Jack nodded and smiled. "Congratulations, that's quite an accomplish…" Jack stopped mid-sentence as he felt the car slow down. Jack looked up and saw the reason why. A roadblock had been set up in the middle of the road. They hadn't seen it before because the only road out of the subdivision curved just as you passed the last house. Then it became a straight away again as it lead to Bremerton. Just passed the roadblock Jack and Phil could see three men standing behind another small barricade. They were in front of a jeep and a large truck, both Army green in color.

Phil stopped the car. "What the hell is that?'

Jack was already opening his door. "I don't know, but I'm going to find out." He turned back to Phil. "You wait here."

Phil just nodded as he stared dumbfounded at the scene in front of him. Jack got out of the car and started to walk around the road block. He looked up to see one of the men about twenty five feet ahead was holding a rifle. Jack heard three shots ring out before he realized the bullets were hitting the asphalt just a few inches in front of his shoes. He felt the chips that flew up bounce off his jeans.

Jack jumped back as his reflexes kicked in. Another man standing next to the shooter put something to his mouth. Jack figured it was some type of bull horn.

"This is Colonel Paxton. You need to get back in your car and turn around. That is an order. Garden Vista Estates and all of its occupants are under quarantine. We have set up our people around the perimeter of the subdivision." Steve Paxton thought of the fifteen soldiers. Four soldiers each on the North, west and east sides and him and three others here on the south. They had the subdivision well covered. "No one leaves until further notice. I repeat you need to get back in your car."

Jack was silent in moment in shock. Finally he cupped his hands to his mouth and yelled. "What's wrong with you? We have a lot of dead people back there. We need some help here."

Again the Colonel's voice sounded. "We are aware of your predicament. There is a radio on the blockade in front of you, take it back with you. We will try and keep you updated on our progress. We have the situation under control, but believe me if anyone tries to leave here, we won't hesitate to shoot."

The colonel put down the bullhorn. Jack noticed that the man beside him didn't put down his rifle.

Instead it was aimed directly at Jack.

As he stepped toward the barricade and the radio, Jack held up his hands in a surrender gesture. He didn't want to get shot trying to retrieve that damn radio. Jack slowly made his way to the sawhorses used in the roadblock. He grabbed the radio off of one and almost dropped it. Jack hadn't expected it to be so heavy. He turned and went back to the car where a pale Phil sat behind the wheel.

Jack threw the radio in onto the seat first, and then he slid in. Phil turned to him. "I can't believe it, those guys really shot at you."

Jack could read the fear and nervousness on Phil's face. "It was just a warning. They weren't going to actually shoot me. Believe me if they wanted to, I wouldn't be sitting here right now." Jack was thinking not yet anyway. He knew better than to share that worry with Phil.

Phil was shaking his head. "What do we do know?"

Jack shrugged. "Right now, we head back to tell the others. Then I think I want to have a little talk with the professor."

Chapter 3

Jack and Phil walked into the clinic. Both men were still shaken up by what they had just encountered. Jack was the more upset of the two. He hated the fact that Phil had been there and seen all of it.

Jack walked over to Bryan. "I think we need to have a talk."

Bryan turned and looked at Jack and Phil. "What's wrong, why are you guys back already?"

Jack shook his head. "Can your nurses watch Mr. Everett for a minute? You and the professor need to come with us. We had better go over to the bar and talk."

One look at Jack's face and Bryan only nodded and went to tell the nurses and get Evan Bradford.

A few minutes later the four men stepped into Jack's bar. Jack turned to Phil. "Maybe you should go and get your dad. I think he should hear this too."

Phil ran out of the bar and over to the hardware store. His mom and dad were both unloading some boxes and transferring their contents onto the store shelves. Phil walked up to them.

"Dad, Jack wanted to know if you could go over to the bar for a minute."

Bob Grady looked at his wife. "Do you mind finishing this up?"

Grace looked from Bob to Phil, she knew something was wrong. "I'm fine, you go on."

Bob followed Phil out of the store. "Is something wrong Phil?"

Phil nodded. "Yeah, but I think you better wait and let Jack try and explain it."

The two walked into the bar. Bob nodded at Jack and Bryan and then looked curiously at the other man before stepping over to Jack. "Phil says you wanted to talk to me."

Pointing to a chair Jack nodded. "Better have a seat Bob; this is going to take a little time to try and explain, if I even can."

Jack started talking, by the time he finished both Bryan and Bob were shaking their heads. Bob was more shook up than Bryan, who already knew about the accident. "I don't understand, why didn't we hear an alarm or something?"

Jack turned to the professor. "What about it professor, you were there."

Evan swallowed nervously. "There was a small alarm, but you wouldn't have heard it. That happened just before the shutdown of the lab at the plant."

Jack stood up and walked over to where the professor sat. "I'll buy that much professor, for now anyway. What I really want to know is what the hell were you and your team really playing with up there?"

Frowning, the professor shook his head. "You already know that BFT is a plant for making new fuels."

Jack reached down and grabbed the professor by his shirt and lifted him up and off the chair. "Maybe that's what we were told, but that's not what you were doing. The army has this place surrounded. We are all nothing more than prisoners here. Now, you had better start talking. Believe me, I'm not the only one in this subdivision who's going to want some answers."

The professor tried to push Jack away, but Jack only got him in a tighter grip. Then he started shaking the professor.

Bryan stepped over. "Hold on Jack, he can't tell us anything with you shaking him like that."

Jack turned to Bryan and slowly nodded and released his grip. The professor fell back into his chair. Jack stepped back. "Okay Bryan, you're right." Jack looked at the professor again. "What was going on up there professor? The truth this time."

Evan shook his head and pulled off his glasses to rub his eyes. He slowly put the glasses back on but only stared down at his lap. When he finally spoke his words came out as almost a whisper. "It was a secret project; no one was supposed to know anything about it."

The men in the bar exchanged glances. Bryan saw Jack once again taking a step toward Evan and hurriedly stepped in front of him and looked at the professor. "Evan, you need to clue us in here. What the hell happened up there? What was this secret project?"

Evan kept staring at his lap a moment longer and then he finally looked up. His eyes were red rimmed.

"We were making a weapon, a biological agent. We've been doing the experiments on several different agents since the lab was built. We were up to our 47th experiment. In fact that's what it was called, BA-47 for biological agent number 47. I don't know what happened. Something went wrong, could have been just about anything. A wrong mixture or something dropped, who the hell knows. That's why the lab shut itself down, that's what the fail safe was for. That's why they're all... they're all..." Evan put his head in his hands unable to finish.

Bryan turned to the others. "Jesus, no wonder the army is out there."

Jack nodded. "And why we are under quarantine." He turned to the professor again. "What's wrong with you people? Your people knew what you were playing with, but what about the other workers up there?"

Bryan too was nodding. "Not only them, how about the whole subdivision. Hell, we have kids living here."

Jack wiped a hand across his face wearily. "The question is what now?" He looked to the others. "I think the first thing we need to do is get the word out to the others in the subdivision."

Jack looked over at Phil. "Do you know where Ben Walker lives?"

Phil frowned. "Our mailman? Yeah, but why?"

Jack sighed. "He must know who all lives in the subdivision and how many. When we know that then we can split up and go tell them what is going on."

Phil nodded. "I'll go get him."

When Phil left, Jack looked at the others. "If anyone wants a drink, the bar's open."

All but the professor stepped to the bar and took a beer. Evan still sat in the chair slumped forward with his head in his hands.

Ten minutes later Phil came into the bar followed by Ben Walker. Ben went straight to Jack. "What's going on? Phil wouldn't tell me anything."

Jack explained as quickly as he could, wondering how many times he'd have to do this. When he told Ben about the deaths in the lab, Ben who had been standing grabbed a chair and sat down shakily. As Jack began talking about the road block, Ben looked up at him. "That was there early this morning. I was on my way to Bremerton to pick up everyone's mail, but I turned around when I saw that."

Jack frowned. "What time this morning Ben?"

Ben shrugged. "Around 6, that's when I always head out."

Jack looked over at Bryan. "When was the accident at the plant?"

Bryan shook his head. "When one of the guys came to get me it was a little after 9. It couldn't have been much before that."

Jack walked over to Evan. "Professor, what time did it happen?"

Evan looked up. "I went out to my car at 8:30. It had to have been within five minutes of that."

Jack glared at the man. "Then what was the roadblock doing up more than two hours before that?"

Evan shook his head as he shrunk back from the look on Jack's face. "I don't know, you have to believe me, I don't know."

Chapter 4

All the men with the exception of Evan sat at a table in the bar talking. Evan sat back in the corner at a different table deep in thought. Something was going on here, something that no one back at the military compound had bothered to share with him or the other scientists he had worked with at the lab for that matter. Evan shook his head at that thought, those he had worked with, they were all gone. He still couldn't wrap his mind around that fact. Not to mention the fact that he should be dead too. Evan looked up when he saw the other men in the bar were standing up from their table.

Ben Walker was talking. "I have some maps of the subdivision at my house and a copy of my mail route. Just give me a minute and I'll go get them."

Jack nodded. "Okay, then maybe we can get something started around here."

Bob Grady also nodded. "While Ben is getting his papers I think Phil and I better go over and try to explain this to Grace."

Phil sighed. "That's gonna be pretty hard when we don't even know what's going on ourselves."

Bob put an arm around his son's shoulder. "We'll figure this out Phil. There has to be some answers somewhere. We just need to find them."

Phil only sighed again in what was more defeat than anything. Then he followed his dad out of the bar.

Looking at the others, Bryan was shaking his head. "Much as I hate to, I better run over and try to explain a little of this to Crystal and Nancy. I want to check on Mr. Everett anyway. I have to tell you I agree with Phil on this one, it's hard to explain something you know nothing about."

Before Bryan could leave, Evan stood up. Bryan and Jack looked over at him; both men had forgotten he was there. Evan nervously cleared his throat. "I wonder if I could say something."

Jack nodded, "But before you do, I owe you an apology for the way I acted earlier. I was upset and not thinking clearly. No matter how or why you ended up at that lab, you were given a hell of a blow this morning. I need to tell you how sorry I am for that and for your loss. Hell, those people were your co-workers and more than likely friends too."

Evan took a deep breath. "Thank you, thanks for saying that. I have to say you were right to be angry though. The others and I on the lab side of the plant lied to this whole subdivision. We knew the danger and by our silence we put all of you in danger. What is bothering me now are those military guys being out there before this so called accident happened. If this was an accident they would have shown up after, not before."

Evan stepped closer to Bryan and Jack.

"There's one more thing you should be thinking about. Why is it a quarantine and not an evacuation? That doesn't make any kind of sense. In the event of a real emergency they should be busy moving people out of here."

Jack stared at Evan as his words set in. The professor was right, but Jack was at a loss for an answer to the problem. "Who's behind that lab over there Evan?"

Evan started to shake his head, and then changed his mind. He had been lied to also and if he hadn't been out to his car at the moment the leak happened, he would be among the dead also. "It's a government operation. About three hours from here there's a military base. It's a secret operation. The actual facility sits a few floors underground. I don't think very many people even knows it's there, not even the military. The place is run by a General William Barlow. The man who is in charge of overseeing the lab is a colonel. His name is Martin Jeffers. He is also a chemist and a psychologist. The government bought up a bunch of land around here when they built the plant. They are also responsible for most of the housing in the subdivision."

Jack frowned. "That doesn't make any sense. Why would the government go to all that trouble and then lie about the whole operation, not to mention endanger all these lives?"

Evan shook his head, but Bryan laughed sarcastically. "C'mon Jack, you're living in never, never land. Our government lies to the people all the time. My uncle used to run sheep down in Southern Utah, ever hear about that fiasco? The bomb testing the government did there and the cover up? All those people dying of cancer, including my uncle."

Evan could hear the bitterness in Bryan's words and nodded. "I'm afraid Bryan is right. Our government is known for their conspiracies."

Jack pointed at Evan. "Then why in the hell were you part of the lab?"

Shrugging, Evan shook his head. "I don't know, maybe because I came to the conclusion that no matter what we did other countries would always have their weapons. That is inevitable. No one is going to destroy a weapon when they feel it gives them an upper hand. So perhaps the best thing, like it or not, is for our country to have the most powerful ones."

The disgust was written plainly on Jack's face. Bryan as a healer didn't know how to answer that. Instead he changed the subject. "Listen, I'll be back as soon as I can and we'll try and make some kind of plans."

An hour later, everyone but Bryan was back in the bar. Bryan hadn't returned from the clinic yet. Ben was standing and the others were seated at the same table they had used earlier. The table top had a large map covering it and Ben was pointing down at it. "As you can see, the subdivision isn't all that big. Over here by the plant is the cul-de-sac where the lab workers had their duplexes."
Ben looked at Evan, but didn't know what to say or how to say it.

Evan just nodded. "It's okay, go ahead."

Ben cleared his throat. "Anyway, there are the few businesses on the main road and here on the east side there's only twenty four houses. Not counting those of us in here and the two families that I know are on vacation. It shouldn't take us long to talk to everyone."

Jack nodded. "Ben's right, if we split up this shouldn't take long."

Evan looked at Jack, his green eyes worried behind his glasses. "Would it be okay if I went along with one of you? I don't want to sit here and I don't feel too comfortable talking to anyone."

Jack shrugged. "Okay by me, you can come along with me. I think Phil and Bob should stay together too."

Just then the door opened and Bryan stepped in. By the look on his face the others already knew what he was going to say.

"Mr. Everett is dead. Those bastards, he needed to be in a hospital." Bryan shook his head. "I told Crystal and Nancy they could go on home. Nancy went to be with her husband, but Crystal will be over here in a minute. She didn't want to be alone. I told Nancy to make sure they stayed in the house and as soon as we got some information we'd be back in contact."

Jack pointed at the map. "You can cross out Nancy's house Ben."

Ben pulled out a pen and put a check mark by Nancy's house, and then he checked off two more. "Those are the two families on vacation."

Jack nodded and turned to Bryan. "We're going to split up the other houses and go talk to them. I guess you can take Crystal with you." Jack looked around at the others. "Just make sure you tell them to stay in their homes. With no phones working that's all they can do and we'll know where they are if we need to get hold of them."

The group all looked at Ben and his maps as he started to assign them the homes that they needed to go to. Jack pointed at the map. "Can I take the southwest corner? I'd like to be the one to talk with Mrs. Carlyle and I can get the other homes while I'm out there."

Ben shrugged. "It doesn't matter to me. If no one else cares."

The others all shook their heads that it didn't and Ben nodded. "Okay Jack, you get the southwest."

Ben finished giving out the assignments and then shook his head. "I still don't understand about the roadblock and quarantine."

Jack tipped his head to the side and then ran his hand through his sandy hair. "I don't think any of us do. I'm just going by what those military guys told me."

Phil slapped his head. "The radio, where's the radio they gave you Jack?"

Jack laughed. "Oh hell, I forgot all about that. It must still be out in your car."

Phil nodded. "I'll go and get it."

He went out the door just as Crystal was coming in. Phil smiled at her and blushed a little. Crystal was a little perky blonde with green eyes and she made Phil's heart skip a beat. He hurried out and Crystal stepped over by Bryan smiling. "I'm done at the clinic and ready. What's the plan?"

Bryan laughed. "I'll fill you in as soon as we get started."

Phil came back in and handed the radio to Jack. Evan stepped next to him. "Be careful Jack, with what's happened today I wouldn't think twice about the government placing a listening device of some kind in that radio."

The others in the room stared at Evan in shock at the suggestion, but knew the chances of that happening were pretty high. Jack looked at the radio, his blue eyes darkening with concern, and then nodding at Evan he turned it on.
"Hello, can anyone here me? This is Jack Carlton; we met this morning at the blockade."

A deep voice came over the radio. "Where the hell have you been? We've been trying to reach you."

Jack rolled his eyes. "Hey, we've had a rough morning here. Who am I talking to anyway?"

The voice came back. "This is Colonel Paxton. I'm in charge out here."

Jack didn't really care who he was, he just wanted some answers. "Well Colonel, we'd like to know what the hell is going on. How long are we under quarantine? We have 23, no make that 24 dead and would like some kind of explanation."

The Colonel's tone was flat. "We know you have some casualties. For now all you need to do is sit tight."

Jack felt like he'd love to go out and strangle this guy. Instead he took a deep breath to calm himself. "We are headed out right now to spread the word to the others. We have to do it personally because our phones are out. I don't suppose you'd know why we don't have any landline or cell phone signals?"

The radio crackled as the colonel came back on. "There was some kind of accident at one of the towers. It's not related to the accident earlier and we are checking in to it."

Jack shook his head. That was just too much of a coincidence to not be related. He knew better to tell the colonel what he suspected though.

"Okay, thanks, we'll get back in touch after we have a chance to talk to everyone."

Jack turned off the radio and looked at the others. He put a finger to his lips and pointed at the radio. "Give me a minute." Jack picked up the radio and carried it out the back door of the bar. He came back in empty handed. "Evan might be right; they could have put a bug in there. I don't want to take a chance either way."

The others nodded as they wondered how they could even have to be dealing with this unnerving situation. Jack was rubbing his hands together. "First things first, let's go share this with the rest of the subdivision. I think for now it's better if we don't tell them everything. Not that we know all that much anyway. I think they need to know not to try and leave. Make sure you let them know that those military guys out there are more than serious. They have no qualms about shooting anyone who tries to leave."

Bryan nodded. "Jack's right, we've had enough deaths around here."

Jack turned to Evan. "You come with me and we can all meet back here when we're done."

The others nodded their agreement and they all walked out of Jack's bar.

Evan followed Jack out to his truck. Both men got in, Jack behind the wheel. When they started off, Jack turned to Evan. "Tell me about this Martin Jeffers."

Evan sat still as he thought for a moment, then he turned to face Jack. "To look at him you wouldn't think too much of him. He's tall, maybe 6'3 and extremely thin. He's balding and combs his hair forward to cover it. Jeffers is a fidgety type. He acts more in need of a psychologist than actually being one. But when he speaks and looks at you with those mesmerizing dark gray eyes everything changes."

Jack nodded. "Do you think he's really capable of setting up what happened out at the plant this morning?"

Sighing, Evan nodded. "I hate to say it, but yes I do. There's something about the man. I won't say evil but I will say something awfully damn close."

Jack was slowing down and pulling up to the first house on their list. "Anything else?'

Evan nodded and pulled off his glasses and wiped his eyes before answering.

"Yeah, Jeffers is in the military and a chemist, but his passion is psychology and especially what makes people act the way they do. I could see the son of a bitch planning this out and setting it up just so he could watch and examine and then analyze people's reactions to the situation."

Jack could feel the hair at the back of his neck standing up, this wasn't looking good. A few more stops and explanations later; Jack was pulling up in front of a house that was different from the others in the Garden Vista Estates Subdivision. First of all this house was older than the others. The Victorian style house was set back from the road and partially hidden by the large cottonwood trees that seemed to stand guard out front.

Jack got out of the truck followed by Evan, who almost reluctantly followed. He looked at Jack. "I'm a little nervous about this one Jack."

Jack smiled. "You've been doing fine so far Evan. This one is no different. It'll be okay."

Evan shrugged and followed Jack to the front door. An ornate brass knocker hung on the overly wide wooden door. Jack reached up and lifted and then dropped the knocker three times.

A moment later an elderly lady opened the door. She was smiling, but her eyes were filled with curiosity. "Can I help you?"

Jack nodded. "Mrs. Carlyle, sorry to bother you. I'm Jack and this is Evan. I own Rusty's Bar."

The woman nodded and opened the door a little wider. "I know the place, not as well as my husband did though. Back then it was called The Tavern and Buck was the owner." Mrs. Carlyle looked from Jack to Evan. "Well, come on in and please call me Helen."

The two men stepped inside. Helen pointed to the far end of the living room they had just walked in to. "Let's go in the dining room, it's more comfortable."

The men followed Helen into the dining room where a large wooden table with six chairs sat center stage. Helen pointed at it. "Take a seat; I was just going to have some coffee. Would you gentlemen care for a cup?"

Evan smiled. "I'd love one, thank you."

Jack nodded. "That does sound good, can I help you?"

Helen waved a hand. "You two just sit here, I'll grab it."

A few minutes later Helen carried in a silver tray with a matching coffee decanter and cream and sugar holders. She sat it on the table. "Just let me go and grab us some cups."

Jack watched her walk out of the room. She almost seemed to glide as she walked and the way she carried herself seemed almost regal to him. He knew she must be in her seventies, but Helen Carlyle moved like she was closer to forty.

Helen brought back three coffee mugs and set them on the table. She looked down at Jack. "Would you pour?"

Jack nodded and stood as Helen took her seat. He poured them all coffee, glad to see that Helen had brought them real mugs and not some dainty cups. Jack hated those things; they never seemed to fit his large hands. Helen added cream and sugar to her own cup and then slowly stirred it before finally looking from Jack to Evan and then back to Jack. "My husband and Buck were close friends. I have to admit they tended to raise a little hell when they got together. Nothing bad really, they just liked to have fun. It's a shame they are both gone now."
She looked at Jack her eyes slightly moist. "I have to say how sorry I am about you wife too, such a tragedy. I knew Rusty when she was young, she was a beautiful child."

Jack smiled and swallowed the lump that had appeared in his throat. "Thank you. She was a beautiful woman too."

Helen took a sip from her cup and then placed it gently on the table. "Now, why don't you two tell me what this visit is all about?"

Jack took a long drink from his own cup, as he tried to decide the best way to share the information with Helen. Jack stared at Helen a moment, she stared back waiting. Jack nodded to himself. "I think the best way to do this is just put all the cards on the table, so to speak."

Helen leaned forward a little in anticipation and curiosity. Jack continued. "There was an accident at the BFT plant this morning. I'm afraid 23 of the scientists who worked in the lab side of the building were killed." Jack looked at Evan. "Evan here is the sole survivor among the scientists over there. Luckily on the other side of the plant where the non-scientific workers were at, there was only one casualty. I'm afraid Mr. Everett had a heart attack and later passed away."

Helen gasped, she knew Mr. Everett. She also knew she should have been more shocked by the other 23 deaths, but the scientists at the lab tended to keep to themselves. Still, she looked at Evan. "I'm sorry for your loss."

Evan nodded and tried to smile as Jack began talking again. "It seems the military has decided to place the whole subdivision on quarantine. We can't leave here until we get an okay from them. I don't know if you've checked, but all the phones are down and if you looked out your back door right now, you'd see that the military has put up a blockade around this subdivision. I was told in no uncertain terms that they would have no problem shooting anyone who tries to leave. We feel it's better if everyone just stays in their homes for now."

Helen didn't say anything, nor did she look all that shocked at what Jack was saying. He frowned. "You don't seem to be very surprised at what I'm telling you."

Helen laughed. "Well, I have seen a lot in my seventy six years. I like to think I am hard to surprise. I have to admit I have been expecting something like this since I sold my property to those BFT people, perhaps not something this drastic, but something none the less."

Jack and Evan exchanged puzzled glances and Helen grinned. "Maybe I should explain myself." Helen took a sip of her coffee, her blue eyes looking intently at Evan then Jack over the cup.

"When I was first approached to sell the property to BFT, I told them no. I didn't like the man they had sent out here. Martin Jeffers is not a likeable man. Anyone who fidgets that much just can't be trusted in my book. However, I finally gave in."
Helen shook her head. "The truth is, I needed the money at the time. Also I was thinking that a few well-paying jobs wouldn't hurt around here either. I hope you can understand that."

Jack nodded. "I do, I didn't work out there, but the ones that did spent their money at my bar and kept it solvent."

Jack thought about that and remembered how before BFT had come he and Rusty were barely making ends meet. They had bought the bar for a song from Rusty's Uncle Buck when he had decided to retire. He had passed away shortly after and never really got the chance to enjoy the retirement he had wanted so badly. Then Rusty had passed away and a short time later the plant had been built and the worker's money had begun flowing in. Rusty had never gotten the chance to see that, although Jack felt she was watching from a better place and would have been happy about it. Jack shook off his thoughts so he could pay attention to Helen's words.

"I suppose the whys don't really matter now. I only saw Martin Jeffers twice after the papers were signed and both times after he left I felt like I needed a scalding shower."

Evan was nodding; he'd gotten that same feeling from Colonel Jeffries. Helen saw Evan nodding. "I take it you know the man."

The laugh Evan gave Helen was more of a grunt. "I've met him; I can't say I know him. I don't think anyone could ever get close enough to really know him."

Helen smirked. "Yes, I got that feeling. The two times he came here to see me he was asking me questions about how people around here felt about having that plant here. If they had concerns about the bio-technologies involved, things like that. I told him maybe he should go and talk to the workers themselves if he wanted to know. All I got from him was that cold smile and that strange stare. He never came back after that second time. I must admit I was glad not to see him again. His questions though left me wondering what he was getting at." Helen laughed a little self-consciously.
"I have to admit I do watch a lot of conspiracy shows on TV."

Jack smiled. "I'm afraid we may find you have good reason to doubt the man and his intentions."

Jack finished the last of his coffee. "Thanks for the coffee and the talk Helen. We really need to get back, but I want you to stay in this house. I don't think we can trust those military guys out there. If we find out anything, I promise we'll be back to share it."

Helen nodded. "I would really appreciate that." Helen walked the men to her front door. "I hope everything works out okay. Myself, I'm old enough it doesn't matter, but I worry for the young people in the neighborhood." She hesitated a minute, then smiled. "And you two stay safe."

Jack and Evan both thanked her and then headed to Jack's truck. Jack drove about a block away before pulling over and parking. He reached in his shirt pocket and grabbed a cigarette. Jack lit it and blew the smoke out his open window before turning a little in his seat so he could face Evan, who was looking curiously at him.

Jack smiled. "I just wanted to go over a couple of things, just you and I. Then we can head back and meet the others."

Evan nodded. "Like what?"

Taking another drag from his cigarette Jack watched the smoke as it floated out the window.

"First, why the secrecy about what the plant was doing? I mean we know it was BA-47 not the bio fuel that caused all this."

Evan shook his head. "Not exactly Jack; remember I was the one who told you about BA-47. If Martin Jeffers and the others pulling the strings had their way I'd be lying dead up at the lab. Being alive I am the wild card in this whole thing." Evan shook his head at the thought of that. "The secrecy is easy to understand. Would anyone have wanted a chemical weapon plant in their neighborhood? I'd have to say no, but bio fuels are the hope of the future."

Jack nodded. "I guess you're right."

Holding up a finger Evan nodded. "One more thing I've been mulling over in my head. For all intents and purposes the Government is still going by the assertion that this subdivision still believes it was the bio fuel that caused this catastrophe."

Jack nodded. "So, I still don't get your point."

Evan shrugged. "Let's say a few of your neighbors drive vehicles that run on bio fuels. Would you be worried? I mean if you thought it was bio fuels that killed the lab workers?"

Jack thought about it. "Yeah, I guess I would."

Evan nodded. "And if word leaked out? A lot of people might be more than a little worried. Maybe they wouldn't want the hybrid cars that used bio fuels or anything new for that matter. The country could just go back to the same old gasoline that is making the oil and gas industry so rich."

Jack's eyes widened as he thought about what Evan was saying. "That's crazy, killing those people so the gas and oil companies can put money in their pockets?" Jack shook his head. "But why the lock down of the subdivision?"

Evan sighed. "That's what worries me more than anything. I have an awful feeling that Martin Jeffers and whoever is in on this aren't planning on any survivors. I don't think they will let anyone get out of here alive."

Jack pulled out the ashtray noticing his hands weren't quite steady and put out his smoke. His old truck was one of the few that still even had an ashtray. He looked over at Evan. "How do you think they'll accomplish that?"

As Evan stared at Jack, his whole body seemed to slump in defeat. "I think they'll blow up the plant."

Jack gasped in surprise. "You must be kidding."

Evan shook his head. "I wish I was Jack, I really wish I was."

Silence filled the cab as both men thought over Evan's words. Finally Jack broke the quiet, unsure if he even wanted the answer to his next question. "What would happen if this BA-47 was released out of the lab?"

Shrugging, Evan shook his head. "I really don't know Jack. The testing on BA-47 wasn't complete. It was made water insoluble, but I don't know what will happen once it gets in the air. Best case scenario the chemical would dissipate, but worst case the chemical may be heavy enough it would float out and land on anything nearby."

Frowning at Evan, Jack was almost afraid to ask. "What would happen then?"

Evan took a deep breath. "If it didn't dissipate the results would be the same as those in the lab. Maybe not as quickly in an open space, but sooner or later I think BA-47 would kill everyone."

Jack shook his head. "Oh hell." He started the engine and began driving. Just before they got to the bar jack looked over at Evan. "Why was BA-47 made water insoluble?"

Evan felt his stomach clench and hoped he wasn't going to be sick as he answered that. "BA-47 was made to put in drinking water."

Evan put his head in his hands as Jack pulled up in front of the bar. Jack felt sick himself as he looked at Evan. A deadly weapon made to be put in drinking water, what the hell was going on? He wanted to tell Evan that it was okay, that he understood, but he couldn't say any of that. What person in their right mind could?

Chapter 5

Martin Jeffers sat in front of his computer, his gray eyes staring at the screen. It was three P.M. He had been here since 6 A.M. The last five hours had been spent watching over and over the same scene.

The scientists in the lab had been doing more working than talking, not surprising; each had been handpicked to participate in the production and experimentation on chemical weapons. They were not picked for their social skills.

A slight smile played across Martin's thin face as he leaned forward.

On the screen twenty four people, most in generic white lab coats went about their business, A few were talking, but most likely they were discussing the project. Martin couldn't tell what they were saying. They had only put in a video hook-up and no audio. He didn't need audio to tell when the short siren had sounded as BA-47 was piped into the room's vents. The look on the scientist's faces easily pinpointed the moment. About half of the people in the lab dropped within a minute. Hitting the hard linoleum floor or slumping over the lab tables or chairs. The others who lasted a little longer

were of more interest to Martin. He wasn't really surprised that only a handful tried to help their co-workers. He did feel he might have enjoyed watching and studying a reaction like that more.
The last to fall was a petite blonde woman. She had smeared the blood that was dripping from her nose and it had left a huge streak of red across her right cheek. Just before she collapsed Martin was certain she had looked straight at him. Her blue eyes were wide and moist with tears. Martin was surprised that she had lasted the longest. He had thought that position of honor would have gone to a bigger, stronger person and he would have put his money on a male also.

Martin began watching the video again and something in the far corner of the lab caught his eye. He had been so focused on his study of the dying he hadn't noticed the movement before.
A dark haired man with glasses was just stepping out of the lab's side door. Martin stared at that spot on the screen until he knew once again all the lab's occupants were dead and the lab sealed as the computer's sensors recognized the danger and put the lockdown in affect. The man never returned.

Martin watched once more to be sure, and then he grabbed his cell phone and punched in a number.

General William Barlow looked at the cell phone on his desk as it played a familiar ring. He grabbed it quickly. "Martin, what's going on?"

Martin didn't bother with pleasantries. "We have a problem at BFT Will."

William gripped the edge of his desk tightly in one huge hand. Everything about William Barlow was large. He stood 6 foot 6 and weighed in at three hundred and ten pounds. Even his shoes were size sixteen. His deep voice came back over the phone. "What's wrong Martin? I thought our people had the place locked down tight?"

Martin had rerun the video and had now froze the picture on the frame that contained the man pushing open the laboratory's side door.
"It looks like one of the scientists got out before we released the BA-47."

The general had let go of his death grip on the table and was now running that hand through his gray crew cut. "Who is it?"

Martin leaned closer to the screen. "I can't see his face. I'll need to review the video until I can get a better picture of him, one where he is facing the camera."

The general's brown eyes were hard. "I suggest you do that Martin and right now. Get back to me with a name as soon as possible."

The General hung up and threw the cell phone on to his desk where it slid across and stopped just before sliding onto the floor. Damn it, he just knew something would go wrong. He never trusted that weasel Jeffers. There was just something about the man, maybe a lot of something's that grated on the general's nerves. Jeffers was a damn good chemist and a hell of a psychologist though. If it wasn't for that he wouldn't have wanted the man around.

Chapter 6

When Jack and Evan returned to the bar, the others were already there. Six pairs of eyes looked up at the two as they walked in. The group had pushed two tables together and were all sitting around it. Bryan waved. "Hey you two, it took you long enough to get back. Hope you don't mind Jack I made coffee. I figured if I started in on beer I might not want to stop."

Jack laughed. "I know the feeling, coffee sounds great. I've been thinking we all could do with some food too. I know that no one will probably feeling like eating, but I think everyone should try. I'll fire up the grill in a minute and maybe fry us up some burgers."

Jack and Evan grabbed their coffee and then joined the others at the table. Jack looked around at the faces there. "I won't ask for details on how this all went right now, but if everyone has talked to your assigned people then I'd like to bring the radio in and call that Colonel Paxton. I don't want the military to think we are ignoring them. In fact I don't want to give them any kind of reason to come in here. Even though right now they have the subdivision blockaded, I'd rather have them around us than in here with us."

Bryan looked around at the others. "I think if anyone would have encountered any problems I would have heard about it by now. Go ahead and get the radio."

Jack nodded and went out the back door and retrieved the radio. He brought it back and sat it in the center of the tables. Then he looked again at the faces that surrounded him. He'd known Bryan and his nurse Crystal for three years, going back to when Rusty had gotten sick. The others, except for Evan, he'd known for five years. He had met them when he and Rusty had bought the bar from her Uncle. No matter what happened he liked and trusted almost everyone in the room. Evan was the only one he didn't know well enough to think that about. Despite his earlier anger at Evan he felt the man might have more to offer than anyone else here. He certainly knew more about not only the plant, but about the bureaucracy behind it. On top of that Jack felt that what had happened this morning was a pretty rude wake up call for Evan. Jack would make a pretty large bet that the Evan sitting here now was a different man than the Evan who had gone to work at BFT this morning. Jack pointed at the radio.

"If anyone else would care to do the talking, it would be okay by me." When no one offered, Jack laughed. "Okay, but if I screw up you'll only have yourselves to blame." He turned on the radio, and they all heard the hiss and crackle. "Hello, this is Jack, hello."

A voice came over the radio, he sounded younger than the man Jack had talked to earlier. But who knew everyone had a story about picturing the person behind the voice and having the image be completely opposite. You just could never tell by a disembodied voice. "Yeah Jack, just hang on and I'll grab the Colonel."

Just over a minute later the more familiar gruff voice from earlier came through. "Colonel Paxton here, been waiting for your call."

Jack rolled his eyes so the others in the room could see him. "We were kinda busy talking to the people around here. We wanted to make sure no one accidently got shot."

The radio crackled. "We don't want to shoot anyone. This quarantine is for your own good. None of us is enjoying hanging around out in this damn heat either."

Jack smiled; he was thinking maybe the Colonel was telling some of the truth. This morning he could have easily shot Jack instead of the road in front of him. "Okay Colonel, I'll just have to take your word on that."

The Colonel's voice came back with a stern tone. "You should really be keeping that radio on and with you at all times. We may have news to share with you."

Jack sighed, he didn't think so. "Right now Colonel, we aren't worried about this radio. All we want is to get some food and maybe try and get some rest, so if we don't answer we'll probably be asleep. It has been a damn long day."

The Colonel stared at the radio he was holding wondering if the people he was talking to knew their radio was bugged. "Okay fair enough. Like I said though, just keep it on and keep it close. We really are trying to help you people."

Jack wanted to laugh, but knew better. "We'll be around Colonel and check back in after we get some rest."

When Jack didn't get an answer back he shrugged and carried the radio back outside. He supposed they could take it apart and look for a bug. He doubted he would know one if he saw it and he didn't want to take the chance of damaging the radio. For now, like it or not, the military guys were their only link to the outside. Jack stepped back in, looked at the others and rubbed his hands together. "I'm gonna start those burgers and I won't refuse any offers of help."

Crystal and Grace stood up quickly. Jack smiled and pointed toward the back of the bar. "The grill is this way ladies."

Chapter 7

Colonel Paxton turned to the man standing next to him. "Corporal, how far do I need to drive to get a cell phone signal?"

The young man pushed back his shoulders and stood up straighter. "Just over a half a mile sir. The top of the first hill going toward Bremerton is the best spot sir."

The Colonel nodded. "Okay Corporal, just relax." The Colonel returned the Corporal's salute with a slight smile. Colonel Paxton turned and walked toward his jeep where he found his first Lieutenant. "I need you to go back and keep an eye on the barricade; I need to go out where I can make a phone call."

The man saluted. "Yes sir."

Steve Paxton got in his jeep and started driving. Steve drove the jeep wishing he was back at the barricade. Better yet while he was wishing, why not wish himself home with his wife. Steve could see the hill the Corporal had told him about ahead. He drove to the top and pulled over to the shoulder. He pulled out his cell phone and checked the signal. Three bars… pretty damn good. It wasn't like he even wanted to make this call to begin with. He hated that arrogant Martin Jeffers. How a jerk like that got to be a Colonel was beyond Steve. Yeah, he knew about chemicals, but in Steve's book, the guy was more psycho than psychologist. He sighed and punched in the number.

Martin Jeffers still sat in front of the computer screen. He'd figured out the identity of the man who had somehow escaped out the back door of the lab. Now he just needed to figure a plan to eliminate the guy. His phone lying on his computer desk started ringing. Martin didn't recognize the number and there wasn't any caller information. Not many had this number. Martin frowned as he answered. "Colonel Jeffers here."

Steve hearing the voice wanted to throw up. "Jeffers, it's Colonel Paxton."

Martin Jeffers felt his anger rise as he looked at the picture on the screen in front of him, blaming the man whose voice he was hearing. "Paxton; what the hell is going on out there? Why haven't you called before now?"

Steve felt his own anger rising. "I didn't have anything to report until now. While you are up in your little computer room sitting on your ass, my guys and I are out here in this damn heat covering your mistakes."

Jeffers was almost screaming. "I don't make mistakes Paxton. Now why don't you just give me your report?"

Steve took a breath wishing he was face to face with Jeffers instead of talking over the phone. "We have the perimeter set up and the neighborhood on lock down. I've talked to one of the men in there; he has communicated to the others the need to stay put. I don't foresee any problems there."

Martin was shaking his head. "Then you don't see a hell of a lot Paxton. We do have a problem. One of those people on lockdown is Evan Bradford and he is a scientist from the lab."

Steve Paxton was surprised at the news. "I thought they were all dead. What the hell does it matter anyway? No one is getting out of there."

Jeffers took a breath to try and calm his nerves; still he couldn't get his legs to stay still. Instead his feet tap, tapped on the floor beneath his computer desk. "It matters a lot if that professor starts sharing information about the lab and the people behind it."

Steve was quiet as he thought about that. He supposed some people could be in a lot of trouble if that information leaked out. He knew he could include himself on that list. "I don't know what you want me to do Jeffers."

Martin was thinking. "For now all I want is for you to keep a close eye on things and keep contact with those guys on the radio. What about the listening device in that thing? Are you getting any feedback on what is happening in there?"

Steve Paxton didn't want to tell Martin Jeffers that somehow those people had known about the bug. That's why they hadn't heard anything and why they couldn't get through the times they had tried to reach the people in the bar. He knew they must have moved the radio out of hearing range. "Not yet, but they were all out talking to the neighbors. From what we could see there are eight people holed up in the bar and the others are going to be staying in their homes."

Martin thought Paxton should know more but let it slide for now. He probably did have more information and just wasn't sharing. He wouldn't put it past him. "Listen Paxton, I've got to talk with General Barlow. Just be ready to make a move when we tell you."

Steve felt like slugging something as he heard the man's arrogance in the tone of his voice. He gritted his teeth. "We ain't going nowhere."

Martin nodded with a smile or what passed for one on his lips. "Okay, I'll be in touch."

Steve was going to answer when Martin's voice came back on the line. "Your men have gas masks don't they Paxton?"

Steve's eyes widened. "Yeah, we got 'em."

"Good."

The line went dead.

Steve stared at the phone a moment before roughly throwing it on the jeep's seat. Damn Jeffers anyway. Steve was almost certain Jeffers was going to ask General Barlow for permission to blow up the plant. Then Steve knew all hell was going to break loose. That stuff they'd been playing with in the lab was some pretty scary stuff. Even for him and he'd seen a lot in his time in the military. It had taken only a few minutes for that chemical to wipe out the lab scientists. Steve thought about what Jeffers had told him. All dead except for this Bradford guy anyway. Steve wondered how that had happened. He supposed it really didn't matter now. That thought made Steve think about the list he had back at the barricade. It had twenty eight names, five of them children. Throw in this Bradford guy and that put twenty nine people down in the subdivision. Jeffers was going to blow that plant full of BA-47 in hopes of killing those people. Then what? Who knew where the chemical would spread to and what kind of damage it would do? Steve Paxton knew one thing, he didn't want to find out and he didn't want five dead children on his conscious. It was time for him to make a trip to the bar.

Chapter 8

Back in the bar the eight people sat around the tables they had slid together. They had just finished putting away the remains of the meal. Now they all had drinks in front of them. They had settled on beer and wine. All of them feeling it was best to stay away from the hard stuff. It was around 6 P.M. The weather outside was still warm and it wouldn't be dark for a good four hours. Jack was thinking about the heat. He knew up in the lab there would be no air conditioning and the temperature would be a lot warmer inside than outside. He hated to think what that was doing to those dead bodies up there. He closed his eyes but when the horrid images came to his mind. Jack opened his eyes and looked at the air conditioner humming in the bar window. Bryan noticed what had caught Jack's attention. He scooted his chair closer to Jack's and spoke in a whisper. "No air conditioner in that lab."

Jack blinked at Bryan's words echoing his thoughts, and then nodded. "You must be a mind reader. That's just what I was thinking."

Bryan tried to smile. "I think we have other things to worry about Jack."

Jack nodded. "I know Bryan, but I just haven't got any good ideas yet."

Bryan placed a hand on Jack's shoulder. "We'll figure something out. I wanted to tell you that if I have to be stuck here with anyone, I'm glad it's you Jack."

Jack frowned and Bryan laughed. "I mean it Jack. I know you aren't going to freak out on me. I can think of quite a few people I wouldn't have wanted to get stuck in here with."

Jack smiled. "The feeling is mutual Bryan."

Jack and Bryan watched Phil stand up and go to the bar's front window. He stood a minute looking out. Phil suddenly turned back to the others. "Hey you guys, we got company. There's a guy coming up the street in an army uniform."

The others stood up and headed to join Phil at the window. Jack reached the young man first. Phil pointed "Isn't that the Colonel from the barricade Jack?"

Jack nodded. "One and the same, wonder what's going on?"

Outside the window, Colonel Steve Paxton held his arms up in a surrender gesture. He spoke loud enough so the people in the bar gazing out at him could hear. "I'm just here to talk. Would it be okay if I stepped inside?"

Jack went over and opened the door. "C'mon in, after we see what you have to say we'll decide if you're welcome or not."

As he stepped in to the bar, Steve half smiled. The cool air hit him immediately and he closed his eyes in the moment pleasure. He opened them quickly knowing why he had come. "I don't know if you'll like what I have to say, but I think the information is something you all definitely need to hear."

Jack nodded. "Fair enough." He pointed to the table. "C'mon in and sit down." Jack looked at the others. "Maybe everyone should have a seat." Jack turned back to the Colonel. "Can I get you a beer Colonel?"

Steve Paxton nodded. "I'd love a beer, and the name's just Steve,"

Jack went over behind the bar, grabbing a cold beer and then opening it out of habit. He came back over to the table and handed it to Steve, who took a long drink. He could feel the ice cold liquid as it slid down his parched throat. Steve sat the bottle in front of him on the table. "Thanks, that sure beats the lukewarm water I've been drinking back at the barricade."

Jack nodded. "Maybe I should make introductions." Jack pointed first at himself then at each person as he went around the table. "Me first, I'm Jack Carlton, I own this bar and of course we met at the barricade and have talked on the radio. This guy next to me is Bryan Hardell, he's the local doctor. Next to him is his nurse, Crystal. Then we have Grace and Bob, they own the hardware store. The big guy there is Ben, our mailman. The young man there is Phil, he belongs to Bob and Grace, and lastly we have Evan."

Steve nodded at each one as they were introduced. When Jack said Evan's name, Steve's eyes widened a bit. "You're the professor?"

Evan nodded and started to say something, but Steve interrupted him. "Before anyone says anything, where's the radio I gave you?"

While everyone exchanged nervous glances Jack laughed. "Oh hell, we must have left it outside."

Steve sighed. "Good, let's just leave it there for now." He saw the curious faces all staring at him. "What I have to say is just between us, my squad doesn't even know the real reason I'm here. I told them I was coming down to see why we couldn't hear you through the listening device hidden in the radio."

Jack nodded his head. "We kinda figured on something like that."

Steve nodded. "I should apologize; I think my being here is my apology. None of this was my idea. Not much of an excuse I know, but I really don't have the time to go into all of it right now. Let me just say my piece and we can go from there."
The others sat waiting and Steve began. "First of all, the man behind all of this is Martin Jeffers, if you don't know him, let me just say the guy is crazy, not a funny, ha, ha crazy, but an evil, dark crazy. He's the one who released the BA-47 out into the lab and killed all of those people."

Evan almost knocked his beer over when he heard that. "Wait a minute; I thought that was an accident in the lab?"

Steve shook his head. "That's what Jeffers was counting on people thinking. He pumped BA-47 out through the vents in the lab, knowing there'd be no questions. Anyone would naturally think the tragedy was an accident, but believe me, that bastard's not done yet. I don't have any of the details yet, but I know Martin Jeffers is getting the okay to release the BA-47 from the lab into the air."

Jack frowned. "How do you know that?"

Steve put his head down and shook it from side to side before looking back up. "Because he asked me if my men had gas masks." Steve heard the gasps and a few exclamations as his words sunk in.

It was Evan that spoke first. "I knew it; Martin Jeffers is more than psychotic. He should be up in that lab room instead of the others."

Jack nodded. "That's probably true, but we need to focus all our attention on what we are going to do right now to help ourselves to get out of this predicament."

Steve nodded. "Jack's right, I for one am not going to let any more people die. I should have done something when my squad and I were first called in. We weren't given the whole story at first either. Now I sure as hell ain't going to order my soldiers to do more killing. Jeffers on the other hand wants everyone dead so no one can tell this story." Steve turned to Evan. "Jeffers knows you got out. He has it on video up on his computer in the military facility he hides out in. Jeffers said you stepped out the door just before the BA-47 was blown in to the lab causing the deaths and the shutdown." Steve shook his head. "You are one lucky guy alright."

Evan was surprised at first, but then he realized that of course Jeffers would have cameras monitoring the lab and the workers. Evan focused back on Steve who was still talking.

"His main concern is that Evan here would tell the rest of you that BFT was actually experimenting with chemical weapons and not the biological fuels you thought they were."

Evan nodded. "He was right, I did tell them. They all know about BA-47."

Steve took time to take another long drink from his beer. "Okay then, we know where we are at. Does anyone have any ideas?"

Evan shrugged; his voice was so quiet you almost couldn't hear him. "I may have something?"

The others looked hopefully at him and Evan held up his hands. "I'm not even sure it will work."

Smiling, Jack nodded at Evan. "Anything you've got going on in that brain of your is a lot better than what's going on in mine, let's hear it."

Evan gave Jack a grin and a slight nod of thanks. "Okay then, I've been thinking about the BA-47. I don't even know what will happen when it hits the air. Jeffers must know more about that than we did in the lab. We had been busy focusing on the possibility of adding the chemical to a water supply. Jeffers must know that the chemical is capable of drifting over and covering the subdivision. He must believe it will retain its potency that far and last long enough to wipe out everyone here. He doesn't want survivors."

Steve was frowning. "We know all that Evan, what's the solution?"

Evan smiled. "I'm getting to that. I think between the hardware store and the small grocery here in the subdivision I can find the materials to make a neutralizer to counteract the BA-47. If we can figure a way to pump it into the lab while it is still sealed, I think we can render the chemical useless."

Steve frowned. "But the lab is locked down. You can't get in."

Evan looked over at Bryan and Jack. "I think we may have seen the place of weakness up there this morning."

Bryan was the first one to understand what Evan was getting at and he smiled. "The window, the one in the controller's room. Is that what you're thinking?"

Evan nodded. "If we cut a hole in there big enough to put a tube in, then we can pump in the neutralizer. When Jeffers opens up that lab the BA-47 will hopefully be harmless."

Bob frowned. "You think you're going to find this neutralizer in my hardware store?"

Evan nodded and smiled. He could feel his excitement rising. "You might be surprised by the variety of neutralizing agents you carry in your store. Things like lime, calcium and plain old baking soda to name a few. I just need to do some calculations to adjust the compound I make and decide on the amounts I will need to neutralize the lab. I'm just not sure how to go about blowing it in."

Bob shook his head and smiled. "If you can do this neutralizing thing, than don't worry about the other. I have a lot of compressors and I think I can rig something up."

Steve was standing up. "Sounds like you all can get started on that. I'll try to find out what Jeffers is doing and when. I'll get back to you as soon as I know anything. Put the radio back in here. Just remember if you talk about any of these plans your making than get away from the radio to do it. My team out there doesn't know about any of this. I think it's better that way. For now all they know is they are supposed to monitor your conversations via the bug in the radio. In fact, they'll be wondering what's taking me so long down here."

Steve started walking toward the door. He turned back to face the others. "I can't tell you how sorry I am about all this. I could say I was just following orders, but that's a hell of a lame excuse. I hope my helping now will go a little ways towards your forgiving me."

With that Steve stepped out of the bar.

Chapter 9

Steve walked slowly back to the barricade. He saw the others had set up a folding table and four chairs. Steve smiled, might as well be somewhat comfortable. Steve was trying to think things through and try to come up with some kind of plan; he also knew he was failing miserably. Everything just kept whirling around in his head. He needed to stop that, if he didn't slow down his mind he knew he'd never be able to focus on the task at hand. Steve sighed as he stepped up to the barricade where one of his men, Devon was standing holding a radio.

"Colonel, we just started picking up those people down in the bar on the radio."

Steve nodded. "I let them know how important it was to keep the radio on and close by, glad they listened to my advice." Steve looked around. "Where are the others?"

Devon pointed to his left. "They just walked down that way to scout around and look for a better view of things Sir."

Steve nodded. "What channel are they using on the radios? Are we still on two?"

Devon nodded as Steve grabbed the radio from him. "Rick, Alex, it's Colonel Paxton, I need you two back at the barricade."

Steve and Devon listened to the conversation that was coming from the people in the bar over the radio while they waited. Steve smiled to himself at the mundane conversation, glad that they knew not to talk about any of their plans while big ears were listening in. Alex and Rick came walking up. Alex was a lieutenant and spoke first.
"Colonel, we didn't find anything a hell of a lot different down that way. We have just as good as a view right here. Did you need us for something sir?"

Steve nodded. "I have to go make a call. I want you three to stay close. When I get back I'll stay at the barricade and have you three run into town for some sandwiches and maybe something cold to drink." Steve was thinking of how easy the cold beer had gone down. If they got out of this mess the first thing he wanted to do was buy a beer for his team and those eight people back in the bar. Steve looked at the three men. "I hope this call won't take long, just hang tight."

Steve smiled when the three saluted. He quickly returned the gesture and then walked to his jeep.

Steve drove back up to place he had called from earlier. Pulling out his phone he stared at the bars making sure he had a good signal. Then he sat a moment longer. He hated calling Jeffers. Steve was sure he wasn't going to like anything the man had to say. Steve laid his head back and took a deep breath before sitting back up and punching in Jeffers number.

Martin Jeffers and General William Barlow were seated in the General's office when Jeffers phone sounded. Jeffers looked at the number with no name on the screen. He knew who the call was coming from as he recognized the number from earlier. Jeffers put the phone on speaker and sat it on the General's desk as he pushed the answer button. "Paxton, that you?"

"Yeah, it's me Jeffers. I wanted to report that we have started receiving the conversation from inside the bar."

Jeffers legs were bouncing as a half-smile came to his face. "Is Professor Bradford in there?"

Steve wished he was close enough to strangle Jeffers. "I haven't heard his name mentioned yet."

Now Jeffers was drumming his fingers against his legs.

"It doesn't matter. He's down there somewhere and by tomorrow morning no one within a mile of the plant will be alive."

Even though Steve had expected it, Jeffers' blunt word still shocked him. "What's going on Jeffers?"

Martin Jeffers smiled across at the General. "I've received the go ahead from General Barlow. At 5 A.M. we'll be remotely opening up the lab. By 5:15 the BA-47 will have reached the subdivision. I have the latest weather report here and between the lab's venting system and the prevailing winds coming in from the Northwest, the project is a guaranteed success." Jeffers sat back in with what passed barely for a smile on his thin face.

Steve was shaking his head. "You sound awfully damn sure of yourself Jeffers."

Martin looked at the man sitting across from him again as he answered. "That's because I am damn sure of myself and so is General Barlow. He's sitting right here if you'd like to ask him."

Steve rolled his eyes. "I'll take your word on it. How long until my squad can get rid of the gas masks?"

Martin shook his head. "You better tell your men to keep them on until you and your team are called out of there."

Steve's brown eyes widened. "How long is that going to take?"

Jeffers was enjoying this. "It will most likely be a good part of the day tomorrow. After the gas is released we are going to wait for two hours to give it time to move to the subdivision and then dissipate in to the air. After that we are going to blow the plant. The explosives are already in place under the building and ready to be set off. I have the remote sitting in my office."

Steve shook his head angrily; he had half expected something like this. "Getting rid of all the evidence Jeffers?"

Martin nodded. "It is the only logical thing to do. You and your men will have to pick up the dead from the subdivision for disposal also."

Steve was seething, but didn't want Jeffers or the General to have the satisfaction of knowing that. He took a deep breath to calm himself. "How long from the time you release the gas until I can send my men into the subdivision for retrieval?" Steve almost choked on the word.

Thankfully Martin didn't seem to notice. He was thinking and now drumming his fingers on the General's desk. "If we release the gas at 5 A.M., you will be able to start grabbing the bodies at 6. You should be easily finished with the pick up before 7 and able to get out of there before the explosives are detonated beneath the plant. Load the bodies in the big truck and move them the hell out of there. You and your team can go back for the mop up after that is done."

Steve stepped out of the jeep and stood looking up and down the road, wishing this was a major highway packed with curious on lookers concerned enough to try and report something strange in the Garden Vista Subdivision. Of course they couldn't even tell something was amiss unless they tried to get in down there. All Steve could see looking both ways on the highway right now was an empty road. Steve started pacing as he talked.
"Okay Jeffers, I got it. At 0-500 hours the show begins. My squad and I will be ready."

Jeffers nodded. "The General and I will be expecting updates Paxton."

Steve was going to answer that, but the phone went dead as Jeffers disconnected. Steve ran a hand wearily over his face and then pressed his fingers against his eyes. How the hell were they going to stop this and help the ones left in the subdivision? How far up the line did this damn cover up go and how was he going to get the word out about this so called catastrophe? Suddenly an idea hit him and Steve stopped his pacing. He punched a number into his phone, hoping Frank was awake. Steve knew Frank always worked the nightshift. Three rings later and the deep, rich voice came on the line. Talking to Frank was like listening to Barry White or James Earl Jones. Frank's deep baritone voice was perfect for his job as a radio talk show host. Frank's show "Your Secret America" was number one in the late night radio market. He had hundreds of thousands of listeners. His voice right now sounded a little cranky. "This had better be important."

Steve laughed. "Hi to you, too."

Frank rolled over in his bed so he could see the clock, 7 P.M. Not too bad, although he would have liked another hour or two of sleep. "Hey Steve, where ya been? I haven't seen that ugly mug of yours in a while."

Steve laughed. "Hey, you're the one who has to be put on the radio so your fans can't see you."

Frank sat up and stretched. "Okay, you win, now what's going on?"

Steve took a deep breath. "There's some bad stuff going on Frank. This one is the last straw. I've seen cover-ups before, but this is one I can't just sit by and let happen."

Now Frank was fully awake. "I take it you think that I can help."

Steve was shaking his head. "I think you're my last hope Obi Wan."

Frank reached into the drawer next to his pad and pulled out a pen and a pad of paper. "Okay, tell me the dirty details, but don't go too fast, I'm taking notes."

A half hour later, Steve drove back to the barricade. He was starting to feel a glimmer of hope. He crossed his fingers that he was right and that involving Frank would gain him the advantage he needed. The men at the barricade turned to watch the Colonel's jeep as he drove in. Steve got out of the jeep and reached for his wallet. He pulled some money out and handed it to his lieutenant. "Dinner's on me, find a sub shop and get some sandwiches. Bring the food back here first. I may have some instructions for you to hand out when I have you deliver the sandwiches."

The three nodded and with their "Yes sirs" and salutes over, they took off for town.

Steve waited five minutes and then called the bar on the radio. "This is Colonel Paxton, is anyone around? Hello, it's Steve."

Jack was the first to grab the radio. "Steve, it's Jack, there's a few of us here. Evan, Bob, Phil and Bryan are out collecting…uh, supplies."

Steve smiled at Jack's choice of words. "That's good; you're going to need them. I talked to Jeffers. They're opening the plant at 5 A.M. According to Jeffers it will only take fifteen minutes for the BA-47 to land on the subdivision. I hope Evan is right about the neutralization. Your people need to have whatever Evan comes up with pumped in to that lab before 5. I think it would be a good idea to tell the others in the subdivision to shut their windows and turn off the air conditioners, and anything else they can think of to keep the outside air out. At least until we see if Evan's little project works."

Jack's face was puzzled. "Is there a way you can find out?"

Steve sighed. "I think so, the Defense, Science and Technology Organization has come up with the M4A1. It's a handheld tester made specifically for biological agents and chemical warfare. If there is anything dangerous that little baby can find it in a heartbeat."

Jack nodded. "Then what happens?"

Steve laughed. "That's probably when the shit hits the fan Jack."

Jack just stared at the radio as Steve's voice came back over the air. "Listen Jack, Jeffers and General Barlow, who is the head honcho up at the military base are going to blow up the plant. They are waiting until 7 A.M. You need to tell everyone to just stay in and wait this thing out."

Jack was getting a bad feeling and didn't think Steve was telling him everything and maybe that was better. "We're really putting our lives in your hands here Steve."

"I know it Jack and I have something in the works. You're just gonna have to trust me on this."

Jack shrugged. "I don't think we have a whole lot of choice."

Steve tried to laugh to lighten the mood, but it came out sounding more like a grunt. "Jack do you have a radio?"

Jack looked at the radio he'd been using to talk to Steve. "I have this one you gave us."

Now Steve did laugh. "No, I mean an AM/FM radio."

Jack smiled at his mistake. "Oh yeah, I got a couple of those, why?"

Steve was thinking of how much of his plan he should share. He didn't want anyone down there to think this was going to be a piece of cake or even that his idea would actually work. Hell, he wasn't even sure of that himself. "When you finish the neutralization, I want you to listen to 94.9 FM. The program starts at 2 A.M. and gets over around 6. I want you to listen and I want the program loud enough that I can hear it over this radio."

Shaking his head, Jack sighed. "Whatever you say Steve. What is the program by the way?"

Steve smiled. "It's called "Your Secret America" and my friend Frank Blazon is the D.J."

Behind Jack, Crystal stood up. "I know that." Crystal made her voice go as low as she could. "This is Your Secret America and I'm Frank Blazon taking you through the night." Crystal giggled and Steve laughed.

"That's the one; make sure you have it on. Now, I gotta go, my guys will be back in a minute. Remember don't talk about anything that might be incriminating." Steve got ready to sign off. "Oh, one more thing, when you get done at the lab you should let me know. Just say something with the word neutral in the sentence. That way I'll know what you're saying, but no one else will."

Jack nodded. "Okay Steve, we'll get it done and we'll warn the rest of the subdivision."

Steve wasn't sure about anything right now or whether they'd be able to get anything done, but knew sharing his doubts wouldn't help. "Okay Jack and good luck, good luck to all of us."

Steve sat the radio down and turned just as the jeep and his three men returned. Steve walked over to the jeep. "Did you guys get enough food?"

Alex smiled. "Yes sir and we got some cold drinks too."

Steve nodded. "Okay, go deliver them and tell the others I want their radios turned to channel three. When you get back I'll be making an announcement. I only plan on going through it once and then we'll have some work to do. So, go ahead and make the deliveries and then get back here so you can have your dinner. Tell the rest of the squad I should be sharing everything in about an hour."

The trio took off and made the deliveries. They returned about fifteen minutes later. Alex handed Steve his sandwich. "We grabbed you one too sir, oh, and you got some change coming." Alex pulled the money from his pocket and handed it to the Colonel. As he pocketed the money, Steve thanked him. He opened his drink, but sat his sandwich to the side.

Alex frowned. "Aren't you going to eat something sir?"

Steve shook his head. "Maybe later, but thanks for going and getting everything and running it."

Alex smiled. "No problem, actually we were glad for the break." Alex looked into Steve's worried brown eyes. "Is it going to get bad sir?"

Steve shrugged. "I hope not, but hell, we've been through lots of different scrapes that were bad and we'll get through this one too." Steve hoped his words were more reassuring to his men than they sounded to him.

A half hour later, Steve looked at his watch and then up to the sky, which was just barely starting to darken. It was 9 P.M.; hopefully it got a lot darker so the people in the bar could get things organized for the neutralization. Sighing, Steve clapped his hands together. It was now or never.

"Okay, I'm ready to tell you guys what's happening." Steve grabbed a radio from the makeshift table; he looked at the three that were stationed here with him at the barricade.
"I'm going to say what I have to over the radio so everyone can hear."
Steve pushed the button on the radio. "Can I get an answer from each of you just so I know I have everyone listening?"

Steve waited patiently while each of his men answered back. "Sounds like we got everyone on board. At 0-5 hundred hours Martin Jeffers under General Barlow's orders will be opening the lab up to the plant. The BA-47 will be released in to the air and be pushed by the fans in the plant and according to Jeffers by the wind and land directly over the subdivision. After I finish my talk, the team members here will distribute gas masks to each of you around the perimeter. I want them on at least a half an hour before the five o'clock deadline. Two hours following the release of the BA-47, the plant will be destroyed by explosives that are already in place. That will be 0-7 hundred hours. We are not to interfere." Steve didn't share that Martin Jeffers' wanted his crew to gather the dead bodies he was expecting from the release of BA-47. With any luck all those left alive would still be that way. Steve continued.

"In the meantime, I am going to open this mic by the radio that is hooked to the one in the bar down in the subdivision. I want everyone and I mean everyone to monitor that frequency and listen to anything coming out of the bar. After the explosion I should have further orders." Steve took a breath. "One more thing, the people in the bar have my permission to move around tonight in order to get their things in order. If you see movement, do not fire. I want those people left alone unless you see them trying to leave the perimeter. Does anyone have any questions?"

Steve waited and a moment later a voice came over the radio, he couldn't tell who it belonged to. "Sir, does that mean everyone in that subdivision will be dead?"

Steve wasn't sure if he should share his plan. He also hoped the squad was thinking about the children in the subdivision, that may help to sway them when they found out he had no intention of following Jeffers' or Barlow's orders. Steve decided the squad would be better off not knowing his plans for now. He pushed the radio button to talk.
"No one knows anything for sure; the BA-47 may prove to not be deadly upon its exposure to the air. Right now, our job is to just monitor the situation. Now everyone should get comfortable. I think we are in for a long night. These three men here will be

bringing out the gas masks. If anyone has any questions about their operation, make damn sure you speak up and ask now. Don't wait until that lab is opened."

Steve sat down the radio and looked at the three men staring at him. "I think we had better go and get that equipment ready for delivery."

The three followed Steve to the army truck wondering what in the hell they had gotten in to this time.

Chapter 10

At the hardware store, Evan was definitely in charge. He knew it and the others knew it, but that didn't mean he had to like it. Every time Evan had to tell someone to do something he'd nervously push up his glasses or take them off and pretend to clean them with the handkerchief in his pocket. Bob, Phil and Bryan had come with him to help get the materials he'd need. Everything they had collected was stacked now on the hardware store's linoleum floor just in front of the one and only cash register.

Evan was standing and looking at the various boxes and barrels they had gathered. Bob stepped up next to him. "I think we found everything you needed. Now, what do we do with it?"

Evan shrugged as he adjusted his glasses for the millionth time. "Well Bob, now I've got to mix all the ingredients together and place it in a container. Then we can figure out a way to blow it in to the lab."

Bob was smiling. "I think this time I'm one up on you Evan." Bob held up a finger.

"Just give me a minute, I'll be right back."

Bob came back pulling a tall cylinder. The tank was on wheels and it had a hose coming out of the top and an electric cord trailing from the bottom. Bob drug it up beside the pile on the floor. "This is the compressor and I've got a sprayer in the back. If I take off the nozzle on the sprayer then we can take the hose and put it up in to the window. That way we can blow this special powder of yours right in that controller's window up at the lab."
Bob slapped his head. "That reminds me, I need to go grab a glass cutter."

Evan smiled. "You do good work Bob."

Bob gave Evan a half bow. "Hey, customer service is my number one priority."

Phil and Bryan walked up to the other two men, carrying an extra-large plastic tote with a lid. The thing looked like it could have been a horse trough. They were both smiling. Phil sat his end down first and pointed at the tote. "Can you use this for mixing your stuff together Evan?"

Evan nodded. "It's perfect, thanks to all of you for your help."

Evan started opening a bag of lime. Bryan stepped over. "Let me give you a hand with that Evan."

Evan nodded and the two hefted the fifty pound bag and dumped its contents into the tote.

Phil stepped up. "If you tell us what to dump and how much, you can mix it up while and we'll dump it in."

A short time later they had Evan's neutralizer mixed up and put the lid on the container. Bob was watching them as he brought the other equipment from the backroom. "We're gonna have to load that tote and this other stuff in either my truck or Jack's. The tricky part will be transferring the dry compound into the sprayer. It will only take about a gallon at a time. I think if we take a couple of buckets we can take turns dumping it in and keep the hopper on top full. Then it can slowly be pumped in to the lab."

Evan nodded. "That sounds great; you all have helped so much. Without you I would have an idea and nothing more."

Bob laughed. "What we did was common sense and common labor. You were the one who figured out the neutralizer."

Evan shrugged. "It was common sense too. Now, I think we should get back over to the bar. I'll be glad to share a little good news." The others agreed on that as they headed for the bar.

At the bar, Jack had found a deck of cards and he, Ben, Crystal and Grace were playing a hand of "Spades".

When the front door opened they all looked up. Evan, Phil, Bryan and Bob stepped in. Jack smiled and stood up. As he did, he pointed at the radio and put a finger to his lips. "Glad you guys are back. Everything go okay?"

Evan stepped over by the table. "Fine, I think we got everything done."

Jack pointed at the door. "I'm going out to have a smoke."

The others followed Jack outside. Bryan was laughing. "Glad you pointed at that radio; I almost forgot we had listeners."

Jack lit a cigarette and slowly blew out the smoke. "That's one thing we don't want to forget. Now, tell me about your work over at the hardware store."

All four men were smiling, but Evan did the talking. "We managed to get the mixture that we'll be using ready. I have to tell you Bob here is a genius. He was the one who figured out a way to blow the powder in to the lab. I'm really feeling good about the possibility we'll pull off this neutralization."

Jack nodded. "I hope so, but I'm afraid there's more. Steve called on the radio while the four of you were next door. He said Martin Jeffers and some General up to that military installation have decided to open up the lab at 5 A.M. to let the gas out."

Evan shook his head and then shrugged. "I guess we knew they would."

Jack nodded and sighed. "There's more, Steve said the plan is for an explosion at the lab at 7 A.M. I take it that they already had provisions in place to do something like that."

Evan was frowning. "Destroying any trace of evidence." Evan thought a moment. "What about everyone in the subdivision? What happens when they find out the BA-47 didn't kill us, I mean if the neutralization works."

Jack let out a breath. "Yeah, that's what I'm worried about. They won't want any witnesses surviving."

Evan nodded. "Especially me, or anyone I may have talked to."

Jack put out his smoke and dropped it in the can that sat next to the bar's front door.

"All we can do is take this one step at a time. You four got the neutralizer ready, that's the first step. Steve suggested we notify the neighborhood to close up their homes and stay inside. That means shutting down anything that is open to the outside air. We need to split up and get that done. Make sure you let everyone know to turn off their air conditioners and cover up any vents."

The others were nodding their acknowledgement as Jack held up a hand. "One more thing, you might also tell them to tune their radios to 94.9 FM to a program called "Your Secret America."

Evan frowned. "What the hell is that?"

Bryan was smiling. "It's a radio program that focuses on Conspiracy theories and Government screw-ups, things like that. It's pretty interesting actually."

Jack shrugged. "All I know is Steve wanted us to listen. So he must have a good reason. Anyway notifying the neighborhood is step two. When we get back it should be time to head to the lab, that's step three. Then we come back to the bar and listen to this talk show and wait."

Grace nodded. "A little praying might not hurt either."

Chapter 11

After delivering messages to the others in the subdivision, the eight person team got busy loading Jack and Bob's trucks. Jack turned to Bob when they had finished. "Bob, why don't you and Grace take Phil and Ben in your truck and I'll have Bryan, Evan and Crystal ride with me.

Jack drove off in his truck first, closely followed by Bob in his. As they drove Jack noticed how eerily quiet the subdivision was. Even this close to midnight, the neighborhood was never this quiet. It gave him a strange feeling, liked he's stepped into an alternate reality or something. He mentally shook himself as he realized they'd reached the plant. He pulled over and parked. Jack looked over at the others who sat in the cab with him. "I guess we can't put this thing off. Let's get going."

Jack and the other three got out of his truck just as Bob and those with him were stepping out of Bob's truck. Jack stepped around to the back of his vehicle and dropped the tailgate. "Let's get this stuff inside."

Fifteen minutes later they had moved everything unloaded from the trucks and into the controller's room inside the building. Evan and Bob were already in the room going through the materials. The others hovered out in the hallway. Jack looked at Crystal and Grace. "Would you two go and block open the front doors, it's really hot and stuffy in here. Maybe you could keep an eye out for any visitors too."

Crystal nodded. "I'd be glad to; I'd rather be out in the lobby than in that controller's room."

Grace was hugging herself. "Me too, I don't like thinking about what's in that lab."

Jack nodded and walked with the women out to the front of the building. "Thanks, both of you. I need to go see if I can help, but give a holler if you need anything."

Crystal laughed; but the worry in her green eyes betrayed her true feelings. "You don't have to worry about that Jack. I'll be screaming my head off if there's even a hint of a problem."

Jack smiled as he turned and headed back toward the room where Evan and Bob were still putting everything together. Phil and Ben had joined them in the small room. They each were holding a bucket.

Bryan was standing just outside in the hallway. "I think I'll just go and join Crystal and Grace for a while. I think they have stuff handled and it's getting a little crowded in there."

Jack nodded. "I'll check with Bob and Evan, see if they need me to do anything. If not, to tell you the truth I'd rather be out front myself."

Bryan turned and headed toward the front of the building as Jack stepped in to the room. "Can I help with anything?"

Bob nodded. "I'm going to cut a hole in this glass. I want to try and leave the piece of window in place until Evan can put the hose up there. When he does I'd like you to put some duct tape around it. Evan is going to hold it, but I'd feel better if it was secured. I'll be running the compressor while Phil and Ben load the hopper with the neutralizer. You might have to spell Evan. I don't know how long this will take, but I do know I want to make damn sure that hose is kept tight against the hole. No matter what, we don't want to take a chance on any of that chemical leaking out."

Jack nodded and Bob handed him the roll of duct tape. Then Bob stepped to the window and used the glass cutter to cut a circular hole.

Bob turned to Evan. "Okay, that piece is just barely sitting in there now. I want you to put the hose up there. As soon as you do the glass should fall out the other side."

Bob turned to Jack. "Be ready with that tape. I'll be turning on this compressor as soon as the hose is up there." Bob turned to Phil and Ben. "Go ahead and fill that hopper now. As soon as we start blowing that powder in you two take turns keeping that holder full of neutralizer."

As soon as everyone said they were ready, Bob pointed to Evan and Jack. "Okay, let's get this thing started."

Evan held the hose in both hands as he stepped up to the window, then he pressed it in to place, watching as the small piece of glass fell away behind it. Jack stepped up and began putting the duct tape around the hose. He could see the white powder as it sprayed into the lab. He could also see the dead bodies lying in the room and was glad it was sealed off; he hadn't to think about what it might smell like in there. Jack was trying to keep his focus on his taping and not on the dead bodies just a few feet away. He couldn't help from thinking that if he looked in he'd see the face of the dead looking back and for some reason an image of his dead wife came to mind. That made no sense, because Rusty had passed away before this damn lab was even built. Common sense didn't help and Jack couldn't shake the feeling. He could feel the goose bumps as they rose on his arms as he put the tape in place. He turned to Evan as he hurriedly finished. "Are you okay if I step out into the lobby and check on the others?"

As Evan nodded, Jack noticed that he too avoided looking directly into the lab. "I'm okay for a while Jack, go on out there."

Feeling more relieved than he knew he should have, Jack nodded. "I'll be back." Jack hurried from the small room and out to the front lobby.

Bryan saw him coming out. "Is that the compressor I can hear?"

Jack nodded; he was still feeling a little shaky about his feelings back in the controller's room and a little embarrassed too. He normally wasn't one to get spooked easily and let things like that get to him. He had to admit to himself that he didn't like the idea of having to step back in to that room. "They've started pumping the powder in, let's just hope it works."

Bryan nodded. "And if it does, what happens then Jack? You know the military and this Martin Jeffers guy aren't going to like it when they find out that the people in this subdivision are still alive after they open up that lab and let the BA-47 out."

Jack shook his head wearily. "One step at a time, remember Bryan, that's all we can do. I'm hoping Steve has something up his sleeve that will help." Jack stepped over to Crystal and Grace who were standing together by the open front door. "Are you two holding up okay?"

Crystal smiled. "As long as I don't think about what or who I know is in that lab I am."

Grace nodded. "Same here, but it's hard to keep out of my mind."

Jack tried to smile. "Well, it's good to know I'm not the only one. It is a little creepy and unsettling in there."

Bryan had stepped up to where the others were standing. He pointed out the doorway toward the subdivision. "Out there too, it just feels too quiet." He looked at his watch. "Even though it's after midnight, you'd expect some noise."

Jack had felt the same earlier and nodded at Bryan's words. He noticed both Grace and Crystal were rubbing their arms. He knew it wasn't from the temperature. It had to be ninety degrees in here and still in the seventies outside. "Listen, I better go see how they're doing. I'll be back to let you know."

Jack walked slowly back down the hall taking deep breaths. He wasn't in any hurry to get back in that room. When he stepped in to the doorway Evan looked at him. "My arms are getting a little tired Jack, would you mind giving me a little break?"

Jack nodded and walked over. "I'll take it Evan, why don't you walk out front? It's a little cooler out there; they have the front door open."

Evan smiled. "Thanks Jack."

Jack took his place at the window and watched Evan walk away shaking his arms. Jack looked at Ben and Phil scooping up buckets full of powder. "How much is left?'

Phil smiled as he dumped his bucket. "Well over halfway done."

Bob adjusted the air on the compressor. "This is really working great, even better than I expected. Another fifteen minutes to a half an hour and we'll be done." He looked at Jack. "How are Grace and the others holding up?"

Jack tried to shrug, but couldn't with his hands and arms up holding the hose, instead he see-sawed his head.

"As good as can be expected, in fact they are all holding up rather well considering the circumstances."

A few minutes later Evan came back in the room flexing his fingers. "I think I can take over now Jack. My arms were cramping a little from being in the same spot so long."

Jack could feel a soreness in his own arms. "I hear you there Evan."

Evan took over at the window. Jack stepped away and then turned back and wished he hadn't. The white powder in the lab floated against the window and stuck here and there. As Jack looked he thought he saw a face pressing against the glass. Jack felt his heart skip a beat. He closed his eyes and slowly opened them again. The image was gone. Jack let out a shaky breath and realized Bob was calling his name.

"Jack, hey Jack, you okay?"

Turning to Bob Jack nodded. "Yeah, sorry, what were you saying?"

Bob frowned at the look on Jack's face, and then shrugged. "I just wondered if you could make a patch out of some of that duct tape, just something big enough to cover that hole. I think we're almost ready to take the hose out of there."

Jack nodded and began tearing off strips of duct tape noticing his slightly trembling hands.

Fifteen minutes later the crew was done in the controller's room and hauling materials and equipment out to the trucks.

Once they loaded everything back in to the trucks, they all got in and headed back to the bar, where no one refused Jack's offer of a drink.

The group all took seats at the table. The army radio sat in the center. Jack glanced at his watch. "Almost time for the radio show."

Jack stood and walked over behind the bar's counter and returned with a radio. Jack turned it on and found 94.9 on the dial. The Eagles were singing about The Hotel California and Jack could empathize with the man in the song. He felt like he had fallen into a place not unlike the one in the lyrics that came from the radio's speakers. He placed the AM/FM radio next to the army radio.

Jack suddenly remembered what Steve had told him to do earlier and he looked over at Grace. "I was thinking about painting the walls in here, what do you think about a *neutral* color Grace?"

Grace frowned. "What are you talking about Jack?"

Smiling at Grace, Jack pointed at the radio. "A *neutral* color Grace, I've heard that a *neutral* color works best."

Grace understood why Jack had emphasized the word and smiled. "Oh, sure Jack, I think *neutral* would work fine."

Chapter 12

At the blockade, Steve heard Jack and Grace's conversation and smiled. He turned to the three men with him. "I need to go back out and make a call. You guys keep monitoring the bar. This shouldn't take long."

Steve stood up and went over to the jeep; he came back to the blockade carrying a roll of black electrical tape. He picked up one of the radios and taped the button for the mic down. Then he spoke in to the radio. "This is Colonel Paxton. I've fixed this radio so everyone out there can get the broadcast from the bar's radio. I want everyone to monitor what's going on down there. Just keep your ears open, you never know what you might catch. I'll be back on here at 0-four hundred and announce a reminder to get those gas masks ready and then again at 0-four thirty when I want everyone wearing those masks. That is one order I won't allow anyone to disobey."

Steve sat the two radios next to each other on the table. He wanted to make sure everyone listened in on Frank's radio show. He wasn't ready to share with his team the fact that he was actually the instigator of the plan. Better for now to let them think those people in the bar started it all. Steve wasn't sure what was going to happen and it might be better for his squad if they were ignorant of this whole thing when all hell broke loose, especially what he was expecting to come down from the military base. Steve got in his jeep and drove back to the spot where he knew he could get a signal for his cell phone. Steve punched in Frank's number. He still had about fifteen minutes until Frank went live.

Frank answered on the first ring. "What's going on Steve?"

Steve smiled, caller ID was amazing. "Hey Frank, I just have an update for you. The people in the subdivision have put some kind of neutralizer into the lab. I won't know until about fifteen minutes after they open that place up if the plan worked or not."

Frank was thinking. "Okay Steve, I want you to call me at 5:30, I can arrange to take a commercial break then and you can fill me in. Will that give you enough time to get back to me?"

Steve nodded, "Yeah, I think I can get back up here and call by 5:30."

Frank smiled. "My show is live until 6, so that will give me the time I need to make an announcement, although by then I plan on already having something in the works. I want to blow this thing wide open Steve. I really hope I can prevent that explosion they're planning at 7."

Steve let out a breath, "Me too Frank, me too. I'll call you back at 5:30."

Steve hung up the phone and just sat in the jeep thinking. He was almost certain that no matter how this all turned out he was done with the army. If he could bring down Martin Jeffers and General Barlow with him, maybe he could take an early pension. If this whole thing went in a different direction then Steve thought he had better take his ass into hiding. Either way he knew he wouldn't be a colonel much longer. Steve started the jeep and drove back to the barricade surprised at how good he felt.

Chapter 13

In the bar everyone listened as Frank's voice came over the air.

"This is Your Secret America and I'm Frank Blazon taking you through the night. I'll open the phone lines in a minute. First let me give you tonight's topic. Everyone has heard about chemical warfare. What I want to talk about tonight is what kinds of chemical's our government is making and just where are they mixing up these agents of chemical warfare. We all know about various laboratories across America where some dangerous stuff is being stored. The big question I have is where are those labs? Are they safe and is this something they should be doing? Just because we know how to do something doesn't always mean we should. The lines are open, let's hear what you think. Go ahead; you're the first caller tonight."

"Yeah Frank, this is Scott in Atlanta. We have a CDC down here and I know they are playing with some viruses that would scare the hell out of you…"

The people in the bar gathered around the table were captivated as they listened to Frank's show. It was one thing to hear someone talk about these things; it was something totally different when you were actually living through them.

At their posts around the perimeter of the subdivision the soldiers listening in were at first skeptical, then interested and by an hour in to the program all were more than a little worried. They knew what was happening down at the lab and this radio show was a little too close to their predicament to not make them wonder what the hell was going on.

Steve sat next to the radio on the table listening to his friend's unique voice and all of the callers concerns. Steve was thankful that he had called Frank. At 4 A.M. Steve picked up the radio and talked into the taped open mic. "Just a reminder, it's 0 four hundred hours. We have one hour until the lab is opened. I want the gas masked being checked now."

Steve waited a half an hour before picking up the radio once more. "Attention, this is an order, I want masks on and I want acknowledgements from each of you as soon as they are in place."

Steve sat the radio down and picked up a pad of paper and a pen. He watched the three men with him put on their own masks; he nodded at them as he placed a check next to their names on the list of his men in front of him. As the other soldiers reported in, Steve also put a check by their names. When Steve checked off the last name he looked at the three men with him at the barricade and slipped on his own gas mask, then looked at his watch. "Twenty three minutes until zero hour, everyone just sit tight."

Steve looked at the radio again and listened to his friend's voice. "...caller 93 is right. A lot of the military bases and labs could be hidden in plain sight. Any one of us could be sitting in a neighborhood and be unaware that some pretty dangerous stuff is being produced. The thing is, it is up to all of us as concerned citizens to be on watch and to get the word out. The people have a right to know what our government, our military and some other organizations are doing. Our health and more importantly our children's health can be in jeopardy. Any chemical or toxic spill is suspect. Why would any of us, knowing our government's track record of lies and conspiracies, believe anything they say? Okay enough from me, go ahead caller 94, what do you think?"

Steve smiled to himself. The callers were getting more and more fired up as the night went on. Steve glanced at his watch again and picked up the radio.

"Five minutes to zero hour. I want everyone to keep those masks on no matter what happens and that's an order."

Steve set the radio back on the table and then stood and walked back to the large Army truck. A few minutes later he came back carrying a black handheld device. It was about four inches wide and eight inches long. Steve sat down and looked at the M4A1; he wiped the screen before turning on the device. The screen lit up with a series of beeps. As soon as the beeping stopped Steve punched in a few buttons and scrolled down until he found the application he needed. When he saw the right screen, Steve stood up holding the M4A1 at arm's length and slowly turned in a circle. The special detector made by the Defense Science and Technology Organization or DSTO showed that the air around this area was acceptable. Steve took a deep breath hoping it stayed that way.

In the bar Jack wasn't the only one checking his watch. If he didn't feel sick, the actions would have been funny. It seemed every few seconds at least one of the eight, who felt imprisoned inside the bar, was looking at the time. At 5 A.M. everyone seemed to be holding their breaths.

On the radio callers were getting more excited as they proclaimed their knowledge of secret labs and government cover-ups. Jack wished they had their cell phone service back. Every person in this bar and in the neighborhood for that matter could really share an interesting story with the listeners of "Your Secret America."

Chapter 14

Steve waited until about ten minutes after five and then he stood holding the M4A1 device. He glanced over at the others. "I'm going to head on up to the lab and check on the levels up there."
His voice sounded muffled beneath the gas mask.

The three men stared up at him. Alex was the first to respond. "Do you want us to come up there with you sir?"

Steve shook his head. "No, just hang tight here. I don't want anyone up there until I know what is going on. I'm hoping this won't take long."

Steve decided to take the jeep; he didn't have much time if he wanted to be back up on the road in time to put in a call to Frank at 5:30. He jumped in the vehicle and drove down the main road of the subdivision that led to the plant. Steve could feel three sets of eyes on his back as he drove off. He drove quickly passed the bar hoping they didn't see him. The last thing he wanted was anyone trying to step out of there to investigate.

In the bar Phil was the first to hear the sound of the engine. "That's a car out there. Who would be crazy enough to go outside knowing they were going to open up the lab at 5 o'clock?"

Jack got up to look out the window, he just caught site of the back of the army jeep. He turned back to the others. "Looks like Steve is going to check if our plan worked or not."

In the jeep Steve was just pulling up to the front of the BFT plant. He got out of the jeep grabbing the monitor. Outside the building, Steve held up the M4A1 and held his breath even though he had the gas mask on. Steve walked around to the side of the building and stepped next to the door where Evan had made his early morning escape. Steve could hear a humming noise and knew the fans were on, expediting the release of gases into the morning air. He could also feel the slight breeze coming from the Northwest that Martin Jeffers had predicted. Steve wondered if the smell of decaying bodies was being emitted into the air as well as the BA-47, and then wished he hadn't had the thought. He was glad for the gas mask. Steve was hoping that the neutralization process might be a help with the other problem as well. He held up the monitor and let out a sigh of relief when no alarms sounded.

The Colonel walked back around to the front of the building dreading what he knew came next. He walked up to the front doors and stepped inside, fighting the eerie feeling that settled heavily on him. Instead of heading for the controller's room where the others had been, Steve headed for the lab. He knew it would be open thanks to Martin Jeffers. Reaching the door, Steve turned the knob and stepped inside. Bodies were scattered everywhere. Steve once again held up the M4A1 and focused his attention on the small screen instead of on his horrific surroundings. He nodded with pleasure. The trace amount of chemicals in the air was not enough to be hazardous. Knowing time was passing too quickly, Steve ran from the lab to the jeep.

Steve stopped the jeep at the front of the bar. He went to the window and knocked. He could see everyone inside staring out at him. Steve motioned his arm for someone to come out, lifting off the gas mask at the same time.

Jack smiled and walked out. He pointed at the mask in Steve's hand. "I hope that means our little project worked."

Steve nodded and smiled back. "It did, great work, but this isn't over yet Jack, not by a long shot. I know you'll want to tell everyone in the bar and that's fine, but will you do me a favor and wait until after Frank's show to share the news with the rest of the subdivision?"

Shrugging, Jack nodded. "I think they can wait a little longer."

Steve drew a breath and nodded. "I think it would be a good idea if you ask them to stay a little longer in their homes when you do share this news."

Jack nodded again. "Done, don't worry we know we're still in a world of hurt here."

Steve patted Jack on the back. "I'm working on that now, just go back in and listen to the radio."

Steve jumped in the jeep and headed out, stopping just long enough at the barricade to let them know that the gas had evaporated and dissipated in to the air and to pass the word it was okay to remove the masks. Then he left to make his phone call. When Steve reached the small hill he held up his wrist to look at his watch and sighed, only a minute to spare. He'd cut that damn close. He used the minute to draw a few deep breaths and steady his nerves. At 5:30 he punched in Frank's number and hit send.

Frank answered right away. "What you got Steve?" Steve smiled at Frank's bluntness.

"The gas is neutralized. They'll still be activating the detonation of the lab at seven and then when they don't hear from me they'll send someone out here to investigate. I think even if I called they would still send out troops. Either way when they get here, believe me they won't want any witnesses. If they find any survivors around here, they won't be survivors for long."

Frank could tell how upset Steve was by the sound of his voice. "Hang in there Steve; I'm setting everything in motion as soon as you hang up. By the way, you might want to catch the end of the show."

Steve nodded. "I'm on my way back now, and Frank…"

"Yeah."

"Thanks man."

Chapter 15

Frank hung up the phone, waited for the commercials to run through and then flipped the switch that put his mic live.

By the time Steve drove back to the barricade, the three members of his squad were seated close to the radio and mesmerized by Frank Blazon's words.

"…and the only reason I've shut down the phone lines temporarily is because it is imperative that I share the predicament of these people. I want everyone listening to me to also share what you hear this morning. If we don't get the word out and fast, a lot of innocent people will be killed. We have been talking about chemical warfare through this show, well right now a secret military base in Montana has released a chemical called BA-47 on a neighborhood of people. Those of you who are constant listeners know this is not a hoax. Just a few miles west of a town called Bremerton is a small subdivision. Their only crime was allowing what they thought was a bio fuel plant to be built in their neighborhood. Instead of bio-fuels this plant has been making BA-47. This Bacterial Agent was intended to be used by the military in chemical warfare. As part of some kind of bizarre experiment this chemical was released at that plant. BA-47 was invented for one purpose, to kill a lot of people as quickly as possible. Thank God some resourceful people have been able to neutralize this chemical. Their predicament however is far from over. Those in charge of this whole fiasco are at the military base that is secretly hidden about three hours from the Garden Vista Estates Subdivision. Those people at the base are not, I repeat are not going to let any of those residents live to be witnesses to what has happened. We, the listeners of this program, as concerned citizens cannot let this happen. I want you to get on twitter, on Facebook, on your blogs. Please, pick up your phone and text or call anyone and everyone you know. We have to get the word to someone high enough up in the Government to stop this horrific act. If you know a congressman, a Senator or even the President himself. Let's get the message out. I've made my own calls, now I am counting on you, and those people, and yes the list includes children, they all are desperately counting on you. Their very existence depends on our help. Remember, this could happen in any neighborhood to any one and we need to let the military and the Government know we won't tolerate it. This is America and we deserve better than this.

Now, I'm going to open the phone lines back up, let me know what you are doing."

Frank looked at the phone sitting next to him all lit up. He hit a button. "Go ahead caller one."

"Yeah Frank, this is Jerry in Detroit. I called a friend of mine who knows the mayor. She's already talking to him."

Frank smiled. "Thanks Jerry, okay go ahead caller two, what's happening?"

Steve and his men listened as the calls continued. Alex looked at Steve. "Okay Colonel, I think you had better fill us in. What in the hell is going on, Sir?"

Steve took a deep breath then shook his head. "I didn't want to say too much before. There's going to be hell to pay around here and I was hoping the less you knew the better off you'd be. If and when something does start happening I thought maybe ignorance might be the best policy. Too late for that I guess." Steve sighed again. "First of all, let me call the rest of the squad back in and then I'll try to explain."

Steve grabbed the radio off of the table. "This is Colonel Paxton; I want everyone back here to the barricade on the double."

Steve sat back and stared at his three men. "I hope as soon as they get here I can explain."

The three men just stared back.

At the bar cheers went up when they heard Frank tell his listeners how some resourceful people had been able to neutralize the BA-47. They were silent however when they realized Frank's other statements were also right. The military or the Government or whoever was in on this wasn't going to want any witnesses. Jack looked around at the worried faces.

"I think we need to be prepared in case this plan of Steve's doesn't work."

Bryan was sitting next to Jack. "Jack's right. Frank Blazon has a large following, but we can't just sit here and wait for a miracle."

Grace nodded. "I'd like to think that miracle would be here soon, but we have to be realists." She turned back to where Jack was sitting. "Do you have any ideas Jack?"

Raising his eyebrows Jack nodded slightly. "I might have a few, none of which will probably be half enough. First though I think we need to talk to the rest of the people in the subdivision. They are in this boat too."

Bob was frowning. "But if Steve is on our side, don't you think he will let us leave?'

Jack shook his head. "Steve probably would, but remember there are people behind this who know who we are and no matter where you go they will find you."

Bryan nodded. "Jack's right and I for one don't plan on looking over my shoulder the rest of my life. I'd rather make a stand here and get this thing over with now."

Jack stood. "Let's go tell the others."

Chapter 16

Two men stood in the lobby outside a large wooden door. Both men looked like they'd just been pulled out of bed and neither looked too happy about the fact. The men were about the same height, but the man with the intense blue eyes was about 25 pounds heavier than the dark eyed man beside him. He pointed at the door. "I don't know about you George, but I'm not looking forward to going in there and sharing this news."

The other man grunted and rolled his brown eyes. "Me either, but hell Dan, you're the head of Homeland Security, you should be used to something like this."

Dan shook his head. "Hardly, what about you? You're the Secretary of Defense George."

George sighed and wiped a hand over his weary face. "You're right, you never get used to it though." Then George shook his head. "Let's get it over with."

Dan nodded and knocked on the door. Dan turned the knob when he heard the voice inside yell. "Come in, it's open."

George and Dan stepped inside and looked at the man seated behind the oversized desk. The man stood and stretched his thin six foot four inch frame. "You two are up early and by the looks on your faces I'm going to regret asking, but what's going on?"

Dan stepped forward first. "Mr. President, we got a problem out in Montana."

The president raised an eyebrow, his blue eyes curious. "Maybe you better sit down; I'll have some coffee brought in."

It took about a half an hour for Dan and George to explain enough for the President to raise both hands in the air. "I think you better let me take it from here. I'll make some calls and see if we can get ourselves out of this one."

Chapter 17

General William Barlow was seated at his desk at the secret military base in Montana. He was disgustedly watching a fidgety Martin Jeffers check his watch yet again. "Damn it Martin, stop it, you're making me crazy. You still have a good half an hour before it's time to set off the explosive."

Martin nodded and then began drumming his fingers on the arms of his chair. "I know, maybe I'll just go back to my office and check on things until it's time."

William nodded his head wearily. "Maybe you better do that Martin."

Just as Martin started to stand up from the chair they heard a knock on the door. The two men exchanged curious glances. The General slid back in his chair, but remained seated. "Come in."

Both the General and Colonel Jeffries looked up as the door opened and two men with MP on their helmets and rifles in their hands stepped into the room and took places on either side of the door.

A man stepped in behind them. It was hard not to notice all the medals decorating his jacket.

General Scott McCarty stepped into the room. His presence alone seemed to fill the area.
"General William Barlow and Colonel Martin Jeffers, by the authority of the President of the United States I am placing you under arrest for the murders of at least twenty four people and the attempted murder of numerous others. General McCarty turned and nodded at two more soldiers who were behind him. They stepped into the room. One went over to where Jeffers was standing and the other walked over and helped Barlow to his feet. They handcuffed both of the men. General Barlow tried to pull away.

"What the hell is this about?"

General McCarty looked at one of the men. "Read them their rights."

Then he turned and walked from the room.

Chapter 18

Colonel Steve Paxton and his fifteen man crew walked together from the barricade down the street to the front of the bar. Steve turned to his men. "Just give me a minute."

The men nodded as they relaxed and took up positions outside the bar.

Steve walked in. He smiled when he saw the pile of assorted pistols and rifles stacked on the table. "You might want to put those away before the President gets here." Steve laughed at the looks that appeared on the eight faces in front of him. "One more thing, do you think I could buy my guys a drink before then too?"

Now Jack laughed as the tension from the morning fell away. "Bring 'em in, but I'm buying."

As Steve went out, Jack turned to the others and pointed at the table. "Maybe we better do as Steve said, I don't think we'll look as innocent if the President comes in and sees those."

BA-47 is dedicated to anyone out there who has experienced their own Government Conspiracy.

I know you are out there.

Once again I want to give out a shout out to the readers who make this craziness I call being an author worthwhile.

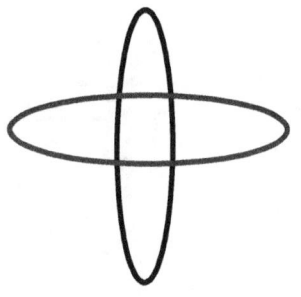